The Changing Labor Market

A Longitudinal Study of Young Men

Edited by
Stephen M. Hills
The Ohio State University

With contributions by

David Ball
Ronald J. D'Amico
Jeff Golon
John L. Jackson
Janina C. Latack
Lisa M. Lynch
Stephen Mangum
David Shapiro

Lexington Books
D.C. Heath and Company/Lexington, Massachusetts/Toronto

This book was prepared under a contract with the Employment and Training Administration, U.S. Department of Labor, under the authority of the Job Training Partnership Act. Chapter 8 was funded partially by the Department of Defense (Manpower, Installations, and Logistics), the Army Research Institute, and the Office of Naval Research. Researchers undertaking such projects under government sponsorship are encouraged to express their own judgments. Interpretations or viewpoints contained in this book do not necessarily represent the official position or policy of the U.S. government.

Library of Congress Cataloging-in-Publication Data
Main entry under title:

The changing labor market.

  Includes index.
  1. Labor supply—United States—Effect of technological
innovations on.   2.   Employment of men—United States—
Longitudinal studies.   3.   United States—Industries.
4.   Insurance, Unemployment—United States.
5.   Young men—Employment—United States.   I.   Hills,
Stephen M.
HD6331.2.U5C47   1986   331.12'0973   85–45710
ISBN 0–669–11943–1 (alk paper)

Published simultaneously in Canada
Printed in the United States of America
International Standard Book Number: 0–669–11943–1
Library of Congress Catalog Card Number: 85–45710

The paper used in this publication meets the minimum requirements of American National Standard for Information Sciences—Permanence of Paper for Printed Library Materials, ANSI Z39.48–1984.

The last numbers on the right below indicate the number and date of printing.

10 9 8 7 6 5 4 3 2 1

95 94 93 92 91 90 89 88 87 86

Contents

Figures and Tables   v

Preface   ix

1. Introduction   1
   Stephen M. Hills

2. The Displaced Worker: Consequences of Career Interruption
   among Young Men   7
   Ronald J. D'Amico and Jeff Golon

3. Adjusting to Recession: Labor Market Dynamics in the
   Construction, Automobile, and Steel Industries   37
   David Shapiro and Stephen M. Hills

4. Adjusting to the Structure of Jobs: Geographic Mobility   63
   Stephen M. Hills

5. Household Costs of Unemployment   79
   Lisa M. Lynch

6. Career Mobility among Young Men: A Search for
   Patterns   91
   Janina C. Latack and Ronald J. D'Amico

7. Long-Run Effects of Military Service during the
   Vietnam War   113
   John L. Jackson

8. Skill Transfer and Military Occupational Training   133
   Stephen Mangum and David Ball

9. How Fluid Is the U.S. Labor Market?   149
Stephen M. Hills

Index   161
About the Authors   165

Figures and Tables

Figures

3–1. Growth in Private Sector Employment by Industry, 1953–73   39

3–2. Private Sector Employment Indexes by Industry, 1973–83 (1973 = 100)   40

6–1. Determinants of Career Patterns   94

6–2. Sample Distribution across Career Patterns   100

Tables

2–1. Group at Risk and Number of Displaced Workers, Including and Excluding Those in Construction, by Survey Year Preceding Displacement   12

2–2. The Risk of Displacement, Including and Excluding Construction Workers   13

2–3. Percentage of Those at Risk in Each Occupation and Industry Who Were Displaced   14

2–4. Extent of Unemployment for the Displaced, Other Job Leavers, and Stayers, Including and Excluding Construction Workers   17

2–5. Wage Differential in Hourly Wage in Period $t + 1$ Following Displacement and Other Job Separations, Including and Excluding Construction   22

2–6. Wage Differential in Period $t + 3$ Following Displacement and Other Job Separations, Including and Excluding Construction   24

2–7. Regression Analysis of Predicted Wage Minus Actual Wage at $t + 1$ and $t + 3$ for Displaced Workers 28

2–8. Probit Analyses of the Probability of Unemployment at Survey $t + 1$ for Displaced Workers 31

3–1. Industry Group in 1978 by Industry Group in 1973 42

3–2. Mobility Patterns, 1973–78, by Industry Group in 1973 43

3–3. OLS Regression Analysis of the Determinants of Leaving 1973 Industry 46

3–4. Unemployment Experience and Receipt of Unemployment Insurance by Industry Group in 1973, Selected Years, 1973–78 50

3–5. Unemployment and Receipt of Unemployment Insurance by Mobility Status and Sector of the Economy, 1975, 1976, and 1978 52

3–6. OLS Estimated Wage-Growth Equations, 1973–78 54

3–7. Joblessness, Job Tenure, and Predicted Values of Wage Growth of Typical Male Respondents, by Industrial Sector, 1973–78 56

4–1. Percentage of Total Sample Reporting Selected Reasons for Moving, by Type of Move, 1976–81 65

4–2. OLS Regression Estimates of the Probabilities of Moving and/or Changing Jobs, 1976–81 68

4–3. OLS Regression Analysis of the Outcomes of Geographic Mobility: Percentage Changes in Wage Rates Ln(Wage$_{81}$ – Wage$_{76}$) 75

4–4. OLS Regression Analysis of Distance Moved, Male Workers, Age 26–39 in 1981 76

5–1. Percentage Distributions of Annual Household Replacement Rates by Race, Household Type, Duration of Unemployment, and Annual Family Income 82

5–2. Logit Maximum Likelihood Estimates for the Determinants of Unemployment Probabilities for Married Respondents 84

5–3. Unemployment Probabilities for Respondent by Selected Characteristics 84

5–4. OLS Estimates of the Determinants of Respondent's Proportion of Time Employed in Survey Year 86

6–1.   Sample Description: Total and by Race   99

6–2.   Sample Description by Predominant Career Pattern   102

6–3.   Standardized Regression Coefficients for Career Patterns   104

7–1.   Sample Sizes by Race and Military Status, and Percentage Distribution of Veterans across Entry Status and Branch   117

7–2.   Mean Values of Selected Characteristics of Civilians and Veterans, by Race and Ability Level   118

7–3.   OLS Estimates of the Determinants of 1976 Wages, by Race   122

7–4.   OLS Estimates of the Determinants of 1981 Wages, by Race   124

7–5.   OLS Estimates of the Determinants of Worktime, by Race   126

7–6.   Accounting for Civilian-Veteran Performance Differentials: Decomposition of Mean 1981 Wages and Worktime   128

8–1.   Percentage of Cases Exhibiting Military-Civilian Occupational Match, by Selected Characteristics   136

8–2.   Logistic Estimates of the Effect of Military Occupational Specialty and Other Variables on the Probability of a Military-Civilian Occupational Match   138

8–3.   Regression of (Ln) Hourly Wage on Selected Characteristics of 1975–78 NLS Cohort of Males: 1983   142

Preface

Since the mid-1960s, The Ohio State University Center for Human Resource Research has conducted the National Longitudinal Surveys of Labor Market Experience (NLS). Five subgroups of the U.S. population were followed over time: women age 14–24 when first interviewed in 1968, women age 30–44 in 1967, men age 45–59 in 1966, men age 14–24 in 1966, and young men and women age 14–21 in 1979. Though surveys are continuing for most of the cohorts, the final survey for each of the two men's cohorts was completed in 1981. Most of the analysis in this book is based on the fifteen years of data gathered for the young men's cohort beginning in 1966.

A total of 5,225 men age 14–24 were interviewed by the U.S. Bureau of the Census in 1966. Sixty-five percent remained in the sample for the final 1981 survey. Personal interviews averaging an hour in length were administered annually from 1966 to 1971 and in 1976 and 1981. Telephone interviews 20–30 minutes in length were also administered to these young men in 1973, 1975, 1978, and 1980. In 1979, a new sample of 6,398 men age 14–21 was interviewed by the National Opinion Research Center at the University of Chicago. The men were reinterviewed annually from 1979 through 1985, when just under 94 percent of the original sample remained.

Funding for each of the NLS cohorts has been provided by the Employment and Training Administration of the U.S. Department of Labor. The NLS cohorts have yielded a wealth of data about specific individuals over time, and because NLS samples are nationally representative, what we learn about them has implications for the entire population.

This book is the last in a series of studies based on the experiences of young men surveyed by the NLS. Earlier Ohio State reports are available from the Center for Human Resource Research in the seven-volume series titled *Career Thresholds*. Since the NLS data have been made public to a variety of users, much work has been done by researchers not associated with Ohio State. The 1985 Lexington Books publication, *The National Longitudinal Surveys of Labor Market Experience: An Annotated Bibliography of Research,* edited by Kezia Sproat, Helene Churchill, and Carol Sheets, cites more than two hundred studies based on the young men's 1966–81 cohort alone.

The original research proposal submitted for this book was mine, but much credit must go to the authors of each of the individual studies, since they carried out the proposed research in detail and elaborated greatly on my original outline. We acknowledge the help of a number of people, although we bear the responsibility for any flaws that still may exist in our research. To Professor Herbert Parnes, who initiated the NLS project, we owe a great debt. We also gratefully acknowledge the guidance and support of Professor Michael Borus (now at Rutgers University), who succeeded Professor Parnes and critiqued the proposal for this book, and of Professor Kenneth Wolpin, who currently directs the NLS. Kezia Sproat provided valuable assistance in editing this book, Carol Sheets's staff made the computer work possible, and Sherry Stoneman completed the word processing both quickly and well. Research associates at the Center provided an ongoing critique of our work: Joan Crowley, Bill Morgan, Frank Mott, Gil Nestel, Elizabeth Peters, and Lois Shaw. OSU colleagues in the Faculty of Management and Human Resources and in the Departments of Economics and Sociology also provided helpful suggestions. Our thanks go to a number of research assistants who made this work possible: Paula Baker, Saeed Kattoua, Edward O'Reilly, and John Thompson. We also owe much to staff members at the U.S. Department of Labor for their ongoing support of the NLS; in particular, to Howard Rosen, who was responsible for initiating the surveys, and to Ellen Sehgal, who served for many years as the Department's liaison for the surveys.

However, we owe the most to the many anonymous NLS respondents who patiently answered our questions and agreed to be interviewed time and time again. We thank them all for their assistance.

1
Introduction

Stephen M. Hills

In 1983, the U.S. House of Representatives held hearings on proposed federal legislation "to facilitate economic adjustment to communities, businesses, and workers; to require business concerns to give advance notice of plant closings and permanent layoffs, [and] to provide assistance, including retraining, to dislocated workers" (U.S. House of Representatives, 1983, p. I). The proposed legislation illustrates a rising concern in this country for economic adjustment to new technology and sharp import competition. During the years of rapid economic growth in the late 1960s and early 1970s, fears about automation and imports were eclipsed by the Vietnam War and Lyndon Johnson's War on Poverty; but in the period from 1979 to 1983, the issues of technology and trade aroused the legislatures of 21 different states to introduce proposals to limit plant closures (McKenzie, 1984, pp. 188–212).

In the 1960s, recessionary periods combined with new developments in mechanization led to the passage of the Manpower Development and Training Act. After passage of the Act in 1962, U.S. training and development efforts shifted to the improvement of the basic skills of disadvantaged workers. In the 1980s, however, policymakers are returning again to issues of displacement, asking how workers may be helped to adjust to new economic conditions.

How many workers are displaced? Even measuring their number is not easy. In January 1984 the Bureau of Labor Statistics (BLS) included in its monthly *Current Population Survey* a special section to measure displacement. According to the BLS definition, a displaced worker was one who lost a job between January 1979 and January 1984, had worked for at least 3 years in the job before losing it, and lost the job because of plant closure, moving of a plant or company, slack work, or the elimination of a position or shift (U.S. Department of Labor, 1984). Prior to the BLS survey, estimates of the degree of displacement were made less directly. Bendick and Devine (1982, p. 184), for example, defined displaced workers as those who on a given date had been unemployed for at least 8 weeks and who were previously associated with either a declining occupation or industry or lived in a declining region of the country.

The BLS calculates that 5.1 million workers met the displacement criterion as of January 1984—about 1 million workers per year. This yearly total amounted to 1 percent of the 114 million workers who were in the labor force in January 1980 (*Monthly Labor Review,* April 1984, p. 60). Bendick and Devine (1982), using their definition of displacement, also concluded that dislocated workers were at most about 1 percent of the total labor force. Though not large in relative terms, this degree of displacement has worried some policymakers because many displaced workers are concentrated in industries traditionally key to the nation's economic health, namely, the automobile and steel industries. Much displacement has also been concentrated in specific communities where broad economic distress is linked to plant closures.

Displacement is not a policy issue if the personal and social costs of displacement are not high, but recent literature implies that the costs can be considerable. Fifteen years ago Peter Drucker (1969) referred to our age as one of discontinuity, and his theme has been echoed by other scholars. In a recent analysis of the development of western technology, for example, Hirschhorn (1984) identifies our time as one in which a new worker-machine configuration controls the production process. The new configuration of work is one of several stages in the elaboration of control over production, and each stage requires new skills from the work force. Hirschhorn and others point out that if the new skills are not acquired, frightening, tragic accidents may occur (Hirschhorn, 1984; Perrow, 1984). Bhopal and Three Mile Island serve as reminders of the consequences of failure to control new technologies with an appropriately trained work force.

The retraining of workers and worker mobility are, therefore, critical processes as changes in technology and in the pattern of consumer demand lead to a restructured U.S. economy. In the United States, both skill acquisition and mobility are, in general, viewed as responses to the decisions made by investors. As technology alters the skill mix of the work force needed for production or as regional cost advantages change and firms shift locations, workers are expected to seek out new kinds of training and move to areas where jobs are most plentiful. Some critics argue, however, that individuals and communities simply cannot adjust quickly enough to the changes that are presently required and that a planned and slower adjustment is desirable (Bluestone and Harrison, 1982). Others argue that we should embrace the changes and improve our capacity to adjust to them as quickly as possible (McKenzie, 1984, Thurow, 1980). All agree that the allocation function of labor markets does not always work smoothly.

This book documents how well U.S. labor markets allocated workers from firm to firm and from region to region in the 1970s. The various studies use longitudinal data to focus on specific points in the working careers of young men when change was most likely; the studies measure the personal costs and benefits of adjustment, and they predict what factors made adjustment easier or more difficult. Although the separate studies do not focus strongly on the process of retraining, one does examine the transfer of skills from the armed forces to the civilian labor market.

The chapters which follow raise a number of specific questions about the process of labor market adjustment. How did young men adjust their careers in a fast-changing labor market and how quickly did they anticipate declining job opportunities in some regions of the United States and move to others? What monetary costs were incurred when young workers were displaced from their jobs and how did unemployment insurance and the earnings of other family members cushion the impact of involuntary job loss? Did the experiences of automobile, construction, and steel workers differ significantly from those of workers employed in other manufacturing firms? What was the impact of the Vietnam War on civilian employment and earnings? How well do skills transfer from military to civilian jobs in the post-Vietnam era? This book addresses all these questions by analyzing a nationally representative sample of young men who were at work during a time of significant social and economic change, all of whom were respondents in the National Longitudinal Surveys of Labor Market Experience (NLS).

The Ohio State University Center for Human Resource Research has been conducting longitudinal surveys under contract with the U.S. Department of Labor since 1966. Two of their longitudinal data sets supply the information for the studies which follow: a national sample of 5,000 men who were age 14–24 when first interviewed in 1966, and a national sample of 6,000 young men who were age 14–21 when first interviewed in 1979. The first of these two cohorts (the Young Men's Cohort) was followed for 15 years, and at the time of these studies, the second cohort (the Youth Cohort) had been followed for 5 years.[1] To help understand adjustment to change in the labor market, each study in this book relies, to some degree, on the longitudinal nature of the NLS data for deriving cause-and-effect relationships.

The changing structure of jobs in the U.S. economy serves as the backdrop for chapters 2 through 5. Chapter 2 examines involuntary dislocation from jobs, an event which was not uncommon for young men because their early work careers spanned two very severe recessions—the recessions of 1974–75 and 1981–82. Even for young workers (age 29–39 in 1981), obtaining new employment following a layoff was not easy. Some of the young displaced workers who were surveyed ultimately accepted jobs paying considerably less than the jobs they had held before displacement, and in many cases, wage erosion did not seem to abate even two years after displacement. For others, however, involuntary job loss did not result in a loss in wages. About one-quarter of those displaced earned more money after an involuntary job separation than before. These workers may have been prodded by their displacement into more remunerative careers.

Chapter 3 compares men employed in the construction industry and in the manufacture of automobiles and primary metals (mainly steel) with men employed in other industries during the late 1970s. First, rates of mobility out of these industries were calculated from 1973 to 1978 and compared with other industries in the manufacturing and service sectors of the economy. Next predicted wage profiles were constructed both for young men who stayed in a single industry throughout this period and for those who changed industries. The predicted wage growth for men who were mobile across industries was considerably less than for men who were not, even after controlling for human capital characteristics. When broken down by industry, young workers in construction showed relatively low wage growth while "typical" young men in the automobile and steel industries showed high rates of predicted wage growth.

Chapter 4 finds that families respond quite directly to economic signals when making decisions to change geographic locations. Several factors were important for men who quit their jobs voluntarily and then moved: the level of unemployment in their original location, the size of the local labor market, and their previous wage rates. A man's family is not less likely to move, however, if his wife participates in the labor force, and the likelihood of moving is not diminished the more his wife earns. All else constant, blacks are less likely to move than whites.

It was expected that government policy would have an impact on the decisions that families make in response to the changing structure of jobs. In the United States the main policy mechanism for offsetting the cost of adjustment is unemployment insurance. This program has been examined quite extensively in recent years for its impact on individual job search and the duration of unemployment, but the present analysis looks at its impact on family decision making. How much family income is offset by unemployment insurance when one member of the household is unemployed? How important is the support of social insurance relative to the earnings that a wife provides for her family when her husband is unemployed? Chapter 5 finds that neither the amount of unemployment insurance nor the amount that a wife earns has a very strong impact on the length of time that a young man is unemployed. Instead, the key factor seems to be the availability of jobs.

Each of the initial chapters in this book addresses a specific problem of short-run adjustment to the market. Yet all these short-run changes could be strongly associated with young men's career patterns over a longer period of time. Chapter 6 turns to a careful examination of career patterns across time but finds that testing for cause and effect is not easy. Because the young men in the sample have widely differing experiences over time, and it is uncertain whether the sum of these experiences should be called a career or not, the authors arrange work patterns over time by means of three different types of career trajectories. They then search for key early experiences and characteristics of individuals which might predict what kinds of careers they may have.

They find that being black still appears to be a substantial liability despite the Equal Employment Opportunity Act. Blacks start out behind whites and show a slower rate of wage growth over time, even when human capital and labor market factors are controlled. Career mobility patterns also differ based on initial choice of an industry and occupational group. Still, being willing to move to the more populated areas of the country where jobs are more plentiful and being willing to go back to school has a payoff for upward movement, regardless of initial choice of occupation and industry. Thus, decisions made immediately following job loss can be important ones.

The most serious career disruption for the men in our study was the Vietnam War, since the youngest men of this cohort were of draft-eligible age during the Vietnam era (August 1964 to May 1975). The long-run effects of the Vietnam War on civilian work careers are not well understood, and documenting these effects is one of the tasks of chapter 7. Veterans of relatively low ability were helped by the service but high-ability veterans were not. Military service imparted positive credentials on white veterans that were recognized and rewarded by civilian employers. For blacks, however, military service was related to less stable employment patterns after leaving the military.

Chapter 8 analyzes the effects of military training in the period following the Vietnam War. In 1982 the military spent more than $10 billion on training, devoting more than 236,000 student man years to its training efforts and making the military one of the largest training institutions in the country (Cooper and Huerta, 1982, p. 39). Military advertising argues that the skills acquired in the all-volunteer army are transferable and useful in civilian careers, but this claim has not been well tested with actual data.

The analysis measures transferability of skills both subjectively and objectively. First, NLS respondents were asked whether the skills they acquired in the military were transferable to subsequent civilian jobs. Second, assuming that similar occupations imply transferability of skills, the military occupations were coded and these codes were compared with the occupational codes assigned to jobs the men held after they left military service. The authors of chapter 8 find that transferability is significantly higher when measured objectively than when measured subjectively. More important than the degree of transferability are the factors which determine which individuals will be more successful in transferring their skills from military to civilian jobs. Race is not a factor, but certain occupations are more transferable than others.

Chapter 9 summarizes the results of the combined studies. To evaluate

Chapter 9 summarizes the results of the combined studies. To evaluate how well labor markets work, the NLS data are compared with other published sources, and the models from each of the chapters are combined to obtain a more complete picture of how U.S. labor markets work.

Note

1. For more information on the NLS see the *National Longitudinal Surveys Handbook,* Center for Human Resource Research, 1984. The young men were interviewed personally in 1966, with follow-up interviews each year through 1971. They were interviewed personally again in 1976 and in 1981, with telephone interviews in 1973, 1975, 1978, and 1980. About 69 percent of the original sample were reinterviewed in 1981. Reasons for attrition were death, refused interviews, and problems in locating respondents who moved. The youth were interviewed in person each year from 1979 to 1984. In 1984, 95 percent of the original sample were reinterviewed.

References

Bendick, Marc, and Judith Radlinski Devine. 1982. "Workers Dislocated by Economic Change: Do They Need Federal Employment and Training Assistance?" In *National Commission on Employment Policy, Seventh Annual Report.* Washington, D.C..

Bluestone, Barry, and Bennett Harrison. 1982. *Deindustrialization of America.* New York: Basic.

Cooper, Richard V.L., and Michael P. Huerta. 1982. "Military Training and Youth Employment: A Descriptive Survey." In R.E. Taylor, H. Rosen, and F.C. Pratzner, eds., *Job Training for Youth.* Columbus, Ohio: The National Center for Research in Vocational Education, the Ohio State University, pp. 39–89.

Drucker, Peter. 1969. *The Age of Discontinuity.* New York: Harper & Row.

Hirschhorn, Larry. 1984. *Beyond Mechanization: Work and Technology in a Post-industrial Age.* Cambridge, Mass.: MIT Press.

Lawrence, Robert Z. 1983. "Is Trade Deindustrializing America? A Medium Term Perspective." *Brookings Papers* 1:129–171.

———. 1984. *Can America Compete?* Washington, D.C.: Brookings Institution.

McKenzie, Richard B. 1984. *Fugitive Industry: The Economics and Politics of Deindustrialization.* Cambridge, Mass.: Ballinger.

Perrow, Charles. 1984. *Normal Accidents: Living with High-Risk Technologies.* New York: Basic.

Thurow, Lester. 1980. *The Zero Sum Society.* New York: Basic.

U.S. Department of Labor, Bureau of Labor Statistics. 1984. "BLS Reports on Displaced Workers." News Release, Washington, D.C., Nov. 30.

U.S. House of Representatives, Committee on Education and Labor. 1983. "Joint Hearing on Plant Closing." Washington, D.C., July 8.

2

The Displaced Worker: Consequences of Career Interruption among Young Men

Ronald J. D'Amico
Jeff Golon

Economic forecasters suggest a substantial transformation of the U.S. industrial structure in the coming decades. With this prognosis comes the expectation that significant numbers of workers will be displaced and will be unlikely ever to be recalled to their previous or similar jobs. The problems these displaced workers are likely to face in their readjustment process and the role (if any) the federal government should play in easing readjustment are questions with which policymakers are already grappling. To help answer these questions, this study focuses on the costs of labor market displacement for a cohort of young workers who were displaced in the past 15 years. We endeavor to estimate the wage loss and unemployment experience associated with displacement and also to determine why some workers adjust more readily than others. Although extrapolating to future years on the basis of the costs experienced by a previous cohort of the displaced is hazardous, these analyses should provide some useful insights and relevant information. In any case, understanding determinants of the costs of displacement has general interest for observers of the labor market.

Substantial displacement of labor in the 1980s could occur as a consequence of a number of trends already in evidence. Perhaps most important, the proportion of the work force employed in durable goods manufacturing is declining. The industries and technologies that have sustained an unprecedented economic boom since World War II are increasingly faced with declining demand, intense international competition, and flat or sagging productivity. The spate of recent plant closings and slowdowns is one manifestation of this decline. Recent projections reported by the Congressional Budget Office (1982) show continued lagging or actually declining growth rates in automobile, steel and related goods manufacturing through the next decade. Moreover, the diffusion of robotics and other microchip technology in these and other industries is likely to cause the displacement of still more workers.

Although continual disinvestment is part of an ongoing process and in fact is essential in a dynamic and healthy economy if capital is to be freed to take advantage of emerging investment opportunities (Schumpeter, 1950), some believe that disinvestment is reaching unprecedented proportions (Bluestone and Harrison, 1982). Estimating the current or projected size of the pool of displaced workers is difficult because of the illusory nature of the concept of displacement itself, but recent estimates place the number of displaced workers as high as 5 million (National Council on Employment Policy, 1983).

For a number of reasons, the displaced are expected to face a difficult readjustment process. Most obviously, displaced workers lose whatever wage advantages accrue to tenure with a given employer. These advantages derive from returns to the firm-specific human capital which workers amass while working for a single employer (Becker, 1975). But besides whatever productivity gains workers realize by maintaining a steady employment relationship, wage returns to tenure also derive from the prominent place wage evaluation procedures and union-management agreements give to seniority in the wage-setting process (Doeringer and Piore, 1976).

Aside from these more obvious advantages of tenure, recent literature emphasizing the continuity of career streams and the importance of timing in career progression also suggests that the wage loss due to displacement may be not only considerable but also enduring. Spilerman (1977) suggests, for example, that the career rather than the single job should constitute the unit for labor market research. In the model he outlines, there are optimal and also disadvantageous moments for job shifts, so some important career decisions are precluded for workers who are displaced. Similarly, Rosenbaum (1979) demonstrates the importance of timing of advancement for eventual career success in his study of promotion patterns in a large corporation.

Finally, fringe benefits, pension rights, and other seniority-related benefits are also thrown into jeopardy with displacement, and the value of these is often considerable.

Not only is much lost with displacement, but the period of readjustment can also be prolonged and difficult. Many dislocated workers have worked for a single employer for a considerable time and hence have only limited job market information and job search skills, which may have eroded. The firm-specific skills they accumulated before displacement are little valued by prospective new employers, aggravating their inability to find new employment, especially at the wages to which they had grown accustomed. This possibility may be particularly pronounced for blue-collar workers because the skills demanded in the continually expanding service and newly emerging high-tech industries may bear little relationship to the ones they possess. The fact that growing industries are often geographically far removed from the industrial heartland, where displacement often occurs, adds a further impediment for workers reluctant to move for financial or nonfinancial reasons.

These considerations suggest that displacement can be a costly experience, as the scant research that exists on the subject suggests. Prolonged unemployment, substantial wage erosion, recurrent employment instability, and loss of pension rights have all been shown to characterize postdisplacement experiences (Mick, 1975; Bluestone and Harrison, 1982). To these must be added psychological costs, as attested by the high rates of mental and physical illness, family breakup, and alcoholism among recently displaced workers (Bluestone and Harrison, 1982).

Although age-specific comparisons of the consequences of displacement are rare, the costs of job loss are often assumed to be borne disproportionately by older workers. Loss of firm-specific human capital and seniority and pension rights, for example, are more likely to characterize the experiences of older rather than younger displaced workers. Part of our aim here is to determine whether the costs usually associated with displacement apply to workers who are still in their 20s or 30s when job loss occurs.

Analyses of the costs of displacement have also been hampered by a number of methodological difficulties, some of which will be corrected here. First, most investigations have relied upon a case study approach. These studies track the short-term subsequent labor market experiences of workers affected by a single plant closing and generally find the costs of displacement to be considerable (see, for example, Stern, 1972 and the studies reviewed in Mick, 1975 and Gordus, Jarley, and Ferman 1981). But those shutdowns which attract the attention of social scientists tend to be of very large plants involving hundreds or thousands of workers. Using such samples may well result in exaggerated claims for the effects of displacement, because layoffs of such proportions are likely to have devastating effects on local labor market employment opportunities and wage levels.

Defining Displacement

Several other analyses have been carried out using national samples of respondents in which a subset of displaced workers is identified. One difficulty with these studies is that identification of the displaced is not unambiguous. Nonetheless some operational definitions of the term "displaced" cause greater skepticism than others. Bendick and Devine (1982), for example, use *Current Population Survey* (CPS) data to identify displaced workers as those respondents who were currently unemployed, had been unemployed for at least 8 weeks, and whose last job was in a declining industry, occupation, or region. The difficulties with this definition are several: because displaced workers are currently unemployed, the effects of displacement on wage erosion upon reemployment cannot be assessed. Effects on unemployment can also not be very well evaluated for two reasons. First, since by definition those displaced must have experienced at least 8 weeks of unemployment, the possibility of a smooth transition to reemployment is precluded. Second, duration of unemployment also remains uncertain because requiring the displaced to be currently unemployed introduces bias by censoring the sample to be studied. Finally, requiring displaced workers to be from declining institutions or regions overlooks the fact that even very healthy environments show evidence of a continuous cycle of deindustrialization, with concomitant reindustrialization elsewhere in the aggregate (Mick, 1975; Bluestone and Harrison, 1982). By focusing only on workers in declining environments, the consequences of displacement could well be exaggerated. In any event, defining displacement in terms of the likely consequences of displacement begs the central question of our inquiry: what are its consequences?

Two successful attempts to identify a displaced subsample of workers use the older men's cohort of the National Longitudinal Surveys (NLS) of Labor Market Experience. The more recent of these (Shapiro and Sandell, 1983) focuses on those workers who were permanently laid off or fired sometime from 1966 to 1978. Over 500 of the over 5,000 sample cases are so identified. In an earlier NLS-based study, Parnes and King (1977) identified displaced workers as being those respondents involuntarily separated from an employer for whom they had worked at least 5 years and by whom they were not reemployed after the separation. They excluded workers employed in construction and agriculture at the time of separation on the grounds that attachment to a single employer is relatively inconsequential for workers in these industries.

Differences in the operational definition of displacement across studies reflect the fact that displacement is an ill-defined concept. For purposes of this chapter, displacement is conceptualized as being an involuntary and unplanned severance from a steady employment relationship, where the prospect of being reemployed by the same employer is unlikely (that is, the separation is permanent), and which occurs to someone who has a strong attachment to the labor force and whose severance is not attributable to the individual's malfeasance. Although several aspects of this definition are impossible to operationalize precisely with NLS data, the following operational criteria reasonably represent the above concepts. To be displaced an employment severance will have to occur: (1) to a worker at least 20 years old in the survey before separation, (2) who was not enrolled in school in either of the two surveys prior to separation, (3) who had at least 2 years tenure with his employer at the time of separation, (4) and was employed in the private sector (government workers and the self-employed are excluded from consideration), (5) who separated for reasons listed as involuntary but excluding being fired (that is, the reason had to be the single category given as "lay-off, plant closing or end of temporary job"), and (6) who was not working for this employer on any survey week job within 3 years after the survey preceding separation.[1]

The notion appearing in Parnes and King (1977) that displacements occurring in construction are different deserves consideration. Craftsmen in construction are prototypic examples of employees in a guild or craft-internal labor market for whom attachment to an occupation rather than an employer is paramount. For such workers, severance of an employer tie is routine and occurs with little cost so long as occupational identification is maintained (Doeringer and Piore, 1976). For this reason many of the results in this chapter will be reported both including and excluding those in construction. A separate chapter of this book (chapter 3) also considers these workers in more detail.

The criteria outlined are applied to all respondents and for each respondent for all survey years between 1968 and 1978.[2] Those who meet the age, nonenrollment, and class of worker (private sector employees) eligibility criteria in a given survey year, t, are examined to see whether they changed employers by the next survey year, $t + 1$. Those who did change employers and had at least 2 years' tenure at the time of separation as well as those who did not change employers and had at least 2 years' tenure by survey year $t + 1$ are jointly called the group at risk in survey year t. Of this group, those who changed employers for reasons given as "layoff, plant closing, end of temporary job" and who did not return to this employer by the survey at least 3 years after survey t (called survey $t + 3$) are labeled *displaced*. Those not displaced constitute the control group for that survey year. This procedure is then repeated for all survey years t between 1968 to 1978. Each respondent could thus be displaced or in the control group one or more times over this period.

Use of this procedure gives us 364 displacements, distributed over the survey years as shown in table 2–1. Excluding those in construction in survey t from the group at risk results in 274 displacements. As table 2–1 shows, the percentage of the group at risk who are displaced varies over the survey years from a low of 1.6 percent to a high of 9.2 percent and, excluding construction workers, from a low of 1.0 percent to a high of 7.4 percent. The consistently lower displacement rates when those in construction are excluded from the group at risk suggests that those employed in this industry have above-average propensities to be displaced.

The year-to-year variation in displacement rates can be attributed to four factors. Most trivially, because some consecutive surveys are at an annual and others at a biennial interval, the period at risk for each survey year t is either 1 or 2 years. Displacement rates should generally be higher the longer the period at risk. Second, variation in displacement rates doubtless reflects period effects to some degree; that is, they are expected to be higher in periods of slack economic conditions. The very high displacement rate for base year 1973 is therefore explicable given the very marked decline in the general economic climate between 1973 and 1975. Similarly, the vigorous years of the late 1960s should be expected to show low displacements, other things

Table 2–1
Group at Risk and Number of Displaced Workers, Including and Excluding Those in Construction, by Survey Year Preceding Displacement

	Survey Year Preceding Displacement								Total Displacements
	1968	1969	1970	1971	1973	1975	1976	1978	
Group at risk	571	666	842	1,293	1,431	1,304	1,530	1,476	—
Number displaced	9	16	22	62	132	21	44	58	364
Percentage displaced	1.6	2.4	2.6	4.8	9.2	1.6	2.9	3.9	—
At risk, except construction	534	624	780	1,169	1,281	1,198	1,418	1,374	—
Number displaced	7	13	19	44	95	12	36	48	274
Percentage displaced	1.3	2.1	2.4	3.8	7.4	1.0	2.5	3.5	—

Note: The group at risk consists of those respondents in each survey year t who were at least 20 years old, not enrolled, and employed in the private sector at time t, who were also not enrolled in survey year $t - 1$, and who had accumulated at least 2 years' tenure with their time t employer by survey year $t + 1$. Those identified as displaced met the same criteria but also left their time t employer by time $t + 1$ for reasons listed as "involuntary: layoff, plant closing, or end of temporary job," and who did not return to this employer within at least 3 calendar years following the time t interview.

equal. Third, the average age of the cohort is increasing over the decade covered by these figures. When slowdowns compel firms to reduce the size of their work force, seniority privileges mandate that those workers with less tenure will be the first dismissed. Since tenure is on average markedly greater for older workers, displacement rates should generally be lower in later rather than earlier survey years. Finally, the number displaced in several of the years is so small that sampling variability must make these rates very unstable. Indeed, the small number of respondents displaced in any single year necessitates our pooling the displacements across all years in all subsequent analyses in this chapter.

An alternative perspective on the prevalence of displacement in this sample is portrayed in table 2–2. This table records in the first row the total number of respondents who appear in the group at risk at least once from 1968 to 1978; no respondent is counted more than once, no matter how many times he is at risk. Just short of 2,800 such respondents are reported. Of this number 343 are displaced from at least one job and 21 of these are displaced from two jobs during this period. Thus, over 12 percent of the at-risk pool suffers one displacement during these 10 years and, excluding those in construction, nearly 11 percent do so.

These percentage displacement figures should not be interpreted as reflecting the risk of displacement in some cohort of workers of the same or similar age in the population at large. First, without sampling weights, the NLS is not strictly representative, because blacks were deliberately over-sampled (use of sampling weights is not feasible here due to our pooled cross-section design). Second, the total employed population in this age range

Table 2–2
The Risk of Displacement, Including and Excluding Construction Workers

Total number observed in group at risk at least once from 1968 to 1978	2,797
Number displaced at least once	343
Percentage displaced at least once	12.3
Number displaced twice	21
Percentage displaced twice	.8
Number in group at risk but not in construction at least once from 1968 to 1978	2,586
Number displaced at least once	280
Percentage displaced at least once	10.8
Number displaced twice	12
Percentage displaced twice	.5

Note: The total number observed in the group at risk is defined to be all those respondents who appeared in at least one of the columns in the row "group at risk" (or "at risk excluding construction") in table 2–1. See the note to table 2–1 for definitions. Those listed as having been displaced twice are also included in the number displaced at least once.

includes those who never accumulate 2 years' tenure with any employer, the self-employed, and those working in the public sector. Thus the employed population is actually considerably larger than the group at risk who are used as the denominator in calculating these rates of displacement. On the other hand, the total group at risk includes respondents observed at risk over only one or a few survey periods before dropping out of the survey, transferring to the public sector, and so forth and who thus have a very short period at risk.

Nonetheless, these figures give some idea of the relative order of magnitude of the rate of displacement among a cohort of young private sector workers over a 10-year period. Judged by these calculations, that risk is not inconsequential.

Finally, in order to describe the pool of displaced workers, in table 2–3 we report the risk of displacement by Census Bureau one-digit occupation and industry categories at the time of the survey just prior to displacement. The column labeled "number at risk" tabulates by industry and occupation

Table 2–3
Percentage of Those at Risk in Each Occupation and Industry Who Were Displaced

	Percentage Displaced	*Number at Risk*
Occupation		
Professional, technical, and kindred	1.8	1,049
Managers and officials, excluding farm	2.4	1,089
Clerical and kindred	3.4	624
Sales	1.1	559
Craftsmen, foremen, and kindred	5.3	2,213
Operatives and kindred	5.0	2,627
Service workers	6.6	226
Laborers, excluding farm	5.6	531
Farm managers or laborers	1.9	162
Industry		
Agriculture, forestry, fisheries	2.3	217
Mining	3.3	181
Construction	12.3	734
Manufacturing, durable goods	3.8	2,630
Manufacturing, nondurable goods	3.1	1,092
Transportation, communication, utilities	3.0	1,254
Trade	3.4	1,665
Finance, insurance, real estate	1.6	379
Service	2.9	918
N	362	9,070

Note: The Number at Risk column tabulates all person-year observations in the group at risk in survey years t from 1968 to 1978. The Percentage Displaced column is the percentage of the person-year observations in each occupation and industry who were displaced by survey $t + 1$. The Number at Risk tabulations represent 2,797 persons observed in the at risk group from one to eight times each.

all person/year observations of the at risk groups from the eight t survey years from 1968 to 1978. The Percentage Displaced column records the percentage of the person/year at risk observations who were displaced by survey year $t + 1$.

As the occupational distributions in table 2–3 show, white-collar workers appear somewhat less vulnerable to displacement and all categories of blue-collar and service workers somewhat more susceptible. Inspection of the industry distributions suggests displaced blue-collar workers are disproportionately drawn from construction; neither of the two manufacturing industries show unusually large rates of displacement. In any event these figures suggest that no group is immune from displacement; both white-collar and blue-collar and workers from all industries suffer involuntary job loss in not inconsequential numbers.

In some sense, though, even this answer is inadequate. Instead of asking who suffers displacement, one might do better to ask which groups are more or less vulnerable during what economic circumstances. The individual survey year data on occupation and industry distributions and related data not shown here, though admittedly unstable due to small sample sizes, nonetheless suggest not only that the rate of displacement varies greatly over time but that the most vulnerable groups vary as well in a predictable fashion with the growth and decline of the various industrial sectors.

The Costs of Displacement

Unemployment Experience

Among the more frequent consequences of displacement is prolonged unemployment in the period following job loss. Table 2–4 examines the prevalence of unemployment in several ways. These are the percentage of respondents unemployed at the first survey $(t + 1)$ following displacement, the percentage unemployed in the survey year $t + 3$, and the mean number of weeks unemployed in the year following the year of displacement. For purposes of comparison similar statistics are reported for two control groups. The first, called "other job leavers," consists of those respondents in the group at risk in survey year t who separated from their employers by survey $t + 1$ but who were not classified as displaced during this period. Most of these respondents were voluntary job leavers, or involuntary job leavers who returned to their survey t employer within 3 years.[3] The second control group, called "stayers," consists of those respondents in the group at risk who did not change employers in the period t to $t + 1$. Recall that by virtue of being drawn from the group, at-risk members of both control groups met the age, nonenrollment, class of worker, and tenure requirements imposed on the displaced respondents.

Turning to the first row of table 2–4, note that over 26 percent of displaced respondents are unemployed in survey year $t + 1$. To aid in interpreting this figure, we show in the second row of the table that on average survey $t + 1$ occurred 8 months after displacement. Although our data do not necessarily reflect uninterrupted unemployment since displacement for these 26 percent, a sizable proportion of displacements appear to be followed by long spells of unemployment.

By definition none of the stayers were unemployed at survey $t + 1$. But the second column of the table shows that those who separated from employer t but were not classified as displaced were much less likely to be unemployed in survey $t + 1$. Among this group only 7 percent of those in the labor force were unemployed and looking for work. Conditions are not appreciably different for either the displaced or other job leavers when construction workers are excluded from consideration. Thus, construction workers who separate are not much less likely to experience unemployment than those employed in other industries, even though changing employers is more prevalent and presumably more normative for workers in craft-internal labor markets.

In survey year $t + 3$, matters have improved considerably for the displaced. By an average 26 months after displacement, respondents are less than half as likely to be unemployed as in period $t + 1$. Although their employment prospects have thus substantially improved, their 10 percent rate of unemployment is still appreciably higher than those of the two control groups: only 4.8 percent of respondents who left their jobs for reasons other than displacement in period t are unemployed at time $t + 3$; among those who stayed with the same employer through period $t + 1$, only 2.2 percent were unemployed. Once again, these figures remain virtually unchanged when construction workers are excluded. Thus by this evidence, displaced respondents are twice as likely as other job leavers and 4.5 times as likely as stayers to be unemployed 2 years after job separation. Not only is unemployment prevalent immediately following displacement, but unstable employment patterns also persist.

Another perspective on the enduring effects of displacement on unemployment propensities is suggested by the final rows of table 2–4. These figures report the mean weeks of unemployment in the year following the year of displacement. To be included in these calculations, respondents must have reported weeks of unemployment (from none to 52 weeks) for a period of 12 months' duration. The second restriction imposed was that this period under observation had to begin at least 1 month but no more than 12 months following displacement. These restrictions were applied to avoid including in these computations workers for whom data were available for only a very short period just after displacement or for only a period fairly remote from the date of displacement; they are mandated by the fact that the NLS does not

Table 2–4
Extent of Unemployment for the Displaced, Other Job Leavers, and Stayers, Including and Excluding Construction Workers

	Including Construction			Excluding Construction		
	Displaced	Other Job Leavers	Stayers	Displaced	Other Job Leavers	Stayers
Survey t + 1						
Percentage unemployed	26.3	7.0	0	29.7	7.2	0
Mean months elapsed from stop date to survey t + 1	8.0	8.8	—	8.3	8.8	—
N in the labor force	350	1,399	7,297	266	1,242	6,816
Survey t + 3						
Percentage unemployed	9.9	4.8	2.2	9.8	4.6	2.2
Mean months elapsed from stop date to survey t + 3	26.4	29.2	—	26.7	29.3	—
N in the labor force	313	1,308	6,854	235	1,162	6,416
Mean weeks of unemployment in the next year	10.3	2.7	1.0	11.3	3.3	.93
Mean months elapsed from stop date to beginning of period of measurement of unemployment	5.2	5.2	—	5.2	5.2	—
N	211	804	3,043	161	720	2,860

Note: Other job leavers are those respondents who changed employers from survey t to survey t + 1 and met all the tenure, age, nonenrollment and class-of-worker criteria of the displaced but did not leave their employer for reasons given as "layoff, plant closing, end of temporary job." Stayers are those who remained with the same employer by survey t + 1. Ns are person/survey year observations. Survey t + 1 is the first survey following separation for the displaced and other job leavers, and the first survey after meeting the criteria for inclusion in the at risk group for the stayers. Survey t + 3 is the first survey at least 3 years after the survey immediately prior to displacement. Weeks of unemployment in the next year refers to the total weeks unemployed in the 52 weeks beginning at least one month but no more than 12 months following separation. For the stayers this period covers the 52 weeks subsequent to the t + 1 survey. Displaced or other respondents whose unemployment was not observed in this period are not included in these calculations. In keeping with the nature of a pooled cross-section design, each respondent could be displaced, an other job leaver, or a stayer in more than one survey period.

have available information on weeks of unemployment for all years from 1968 to 1980 nor can spells of unemployment be precisely dated.

With these restrictions imposed, the results show the displaced suffer on average just over 10 weeks of unemployment out of the 52 weeks considered. In a pattern that is by now quite familiar, members of both control groups suffer substantially less unemployment: 2.7 weeks for other job changers and just 1 week for stayers. For both groups of job changers the period considered begins on average 5.2 months after separation.

Perhaps the most interesting statistic (not shown in table 2–4) is the percentage of displacements followed immediately by some unemployment. Such a figure would enable us to identify those cases where workers, presumably with advance warning of impending displacement, were able to line up alternative employment to commence when their current job ended. Unfortunately, the lack of any unemployment data for some years covered by the NLS, and our inability to precisely date those spells of unemployment which are reported, cause this statistic to be unavailable in most instances. As a proxy, we did identify a subset of cases for which amount of unemployment could be ascertained for the period continuous from displacement to the next survey. Of the 364 displacements, 234 had such information available. The data show that 63 percent of these cases had at least 1 week of unemployment reported during this period. By this measure, then, the majority of displacements are followed by at least some disruption and job search, but almost two-fifths were not unemployed.

Wage Loss Following Displacement

Wage loss is a second consequence commonly associated with displacement. Most investigations of this outcome, as with unemployment, have been conducted on samples of older workers (Parnes and King, 1977; Shapiro and Sandell, 1983) or on a cross-section of workers employed in a plant suffering a shutdown, most of whom can be expected to have had lengthy employment tenures. Among these samples of workers, the wage loss associated with displacement was found to be considerable. The present study, focusing on workers who are no older than their 20s or 30s, enables us to investigate the robustness of these earlier conclusions. By the time of displacement, younger workers should have invested less heavily in firm-specific human capital and other nontransferable skills than older workers, and their general human capital should not have had time to be seriously eroded. Younger workers also have generally invested less heavily both psychically and financially in their homes and communities and hence should be more geographically mobile in pursuit of attractive employment opportunities. For these reasons one would expect a younger cohort of workers to fare substantially better when wage loss following displacement is considered. Other considerations, too, including age discrimination by employers and willingness of younger employees to invest in new skills should also work to favor the young. For all these reasons we might expect the cost of displacement for these workers to be less severe than has commonly been observed.

At the same time the wage loss even for these young workers might be considerable. Even very young workers often make considerable investments in firm-specific skills, and the early years of one's career are often considered the most critical as workers try to establish footholds in organizational hierarchies. These considerations suggest not only that wage loss immediately after displacement might be substantial but also that the disadvantages incurred may be enduring as well. The extent of wage loss following displacement, then, and the question to which it gives rise—What causes some displaced workers to fare better than others?—are the issues addressed in the following sections.

A variety of methodologies could be employed in addressing the wage loss issue and a variety have been tried in the literature.[4] The approach used here is conceptually quite similar to a pooled cross-section where wage on survey $t + 1$ is regressed on predisplacement wage t, control variables, and a dummy variable for whether the respondent was displaced between t and $t + 1$. We depart from a pooled cross-section design by not assuming that the determinants of wage growth or the effects of displacement are constant across all periods. In essence, we will compute a predicted wage for displaced respondents in the first year ($t + 1$) and third year ($t + 3$) after displacement (with the survey just prior to displacement labeled "period t") on the basis of predisplacement wages and other characteristics of respondents. The mean differential between predicted and actual wages in the postdisplacement periods will be interpreted as being due to displacement. The prediction equations will be estimated on the basis of coefficients generated from the sample of nondisplaced respondents who meet the age, nonenrollment, and other restrictions used in defining the displaced sample (that is, those in the control group). To control for period effects in wage growth over the eight "period t" surveys covered by the data, these prediction equations are generated separately for those displaced in each of the eight periods, using coefficients generated from equations estimated separately for those in each of the eight control groups.[5]

Specifically, for those in the group at risk at each period t who were not displaced by $t + 1$ and who had valid data on relevant variables, we regress $t + 1$ wage (adjusted to 1981 dollars) on: period t and period $t - 1$ hourly wages (both in 1981 dollars) and, to allow different wage-growth profiles for those with different characteristics, years of education at time $t + 1$, age, tenure with employer at time $t + 1$, a dummy variable for whether the respondent lived in a Standard Metropolitan Statistical Area (SMSA) at time $t + 1$, and a second dummy variable for the respondent's race. The point of these analyses was not to produce necessarily meaningful or interpretable coefficients but to generate as high a set of R-squareds as possible so that when applied to the sample of displaced workers these equations will lead to predicted wages in which we can have high confidence. In general, these R-squareds for the control group wage-growth equations are quite high, generally approaching or exceeding .70 for most of the eight t survey years.

This procedure is then repeated, again using those in the control group at each survey t, except that wage at $t + 3$ is dependent and regressed on the same independent variables but with tenure, education, and SMSA residence measured as of time $t + 3$. R-squareds from these equations are lower but still satisfactory.

Those displaced between each period t to $t + 1$ then have their $t + 1$ and $t + 3$ hourly wages predicted using the coefficients from the relevant equations for those in the time t control group. However, for displaced respondents education and SMSA residence are measured as of time t because subsequent education or residence may be endogenous to displacement. Also, tenure is imputed assuming no interruption of the employment relationship by time $t + 1$ or time $t + 3$ (that is, tenure as of the time of separation is added to time elapsed since the separation). The results of these procedures should be predicted $t + 1$ and $t + 3$ wages for displaced respondents in the absence of displacement, assuming they had not separated from their employers, that their time t attributes of education and residence remained unchanged and that their wage growth would have been similar to those in the control group who had similar characteristics over the same period.[6]

The difference between their predicted $t + 1$ or $t + 3$ wages and their actual wages for these periods then represents the wage loss (or gain) associated with displacement.[7] Because period differences in the extent of wage growth are effectively controlled by these procedures, measures of wage loss or gain can be averaged across the eight base year surveys.

Before presenting results of these calculations one caution is in order. Results of these procedures may actually seriously understate the true wage loss following displacement, because only those displaced respondents who were reemployed by survey $t + 1$ or $t + 3$ can be included in these computations. In 14 of the 364 displacements, the displaced worker dropped out of the labor force by survey $t + 1$. Over one-quarter of the remaining respondents were unemployed by survey $t + 1$, as table 2–4 has shown. Those who were unemployed or out of the labor force at survey $t + 1$ might well include those who had the hardest time finding reemployment at anything approaching their predisplacement wage. Failure to include these respondents in the $t + 1$ wage loss calculations might give a less unfavorable portrait of the postdisplacement mean wage loss than is warranted. Less of a problem is suggested for the $t + 3$ wage calculations, because fewer of the displaced were unemployed on that survey date.

With these caveats in mind, we show results in table 2–5 for the wage differential estimates in period $t + 1$ and in table 2–6 for estimates in period $t + 3$. In addition to showing results for displaced workers, these tables also show, for purposes of comparison, results for respondents in the control group who changed employers from period t to $t + 1$, as well as for the total control group.

As table 2–5 shows, the wage differential for displaced workers at period $t + 1$ is a loss of over 58 cents an hour, not inconsiderable but also not as large as might have been expected. When workers employed in construction in the survey before displacement are excluded from these calculations, the estimated wage loss jumps to nearly 73 cents. By contrast, the corresponding losses for other job separators including and excluding those in construction are 14 cents and 12 cents, respectively. Thus, those displaced fare considerably worse than other job leavers. To put these figures in perspective, we show in the bottom row of table 2–5 the mean time elapsed from displacement or other separation to the survey $t + 1$ when the wage loss is calculated. The mean time for recovery is shown to be between about 8 and 9 months. Thus, about two-thirds of a year after losing their jobs, displaced workers who were not in construction earned 72 cents an hour less than they might have expected had they not lost their jobs. Because the mean wage for this sample is about $7.85 per hour over this period, these figures represent about a 9.2 percent loss in earnings capacity.

Table 2–5 shows there is also considerable variance in fortunes following displacement. Nearly 20 percent of those displaced lose more than $2.50 per hour following displacement and nearly half of those displaced lose $1.00 or more. Thus, for a considerable number of displaced workers, readjustment is difficult and is accompanied by a substantial loss in earning power. At the same time, a number of displaced workers are able to improve their labor market position quite noticeably following displacement; about one-quarter of those displaced see their hourly wage increase by more than $1.00 over their projected earnings stream. Thus, the 59 cent or 73 cent mean wage loss following displacement masks the fact that many workers suffer quite severely while others suffer little loss or even gain handsomely from their employment separation. Federal efforts aimed at helping the displaced should take note of this fact; ideally relocation assistance should be targeted to only a subset of the displaced.

Part of the variance in the wage differential for the displaced doubtless reflects the fact that predisplacement wages, and hence postdisplacement wage projections, are measured with error. Moreover, even in the absence of displacement, some of these workers would have realized a large wage gain or loss by virtue of their being promoted or demoted. The distribution of the wage differentials for the control group therefore helps put the figures for the displaced into perspective. As table 2–5 shows, the displaced are only slightly

Table 2–5
Wage Differential in Hourly Wage in Period t + 1 Following Displacement and Other Job Separations, Including and Excluding Construction

	Including Construction			Excluding Construction		
	Displacements	Other Job Separations	Total Control Group	Displacements	Other Job Separations	Total Control Group
Mean wage differential in hourly wage in cents at t + 1	58.5	14.0	0.0	72.9	12.3	1.8
Percentage losing or gaining						
$2.50 or more loss	18.6	16.2	6.8	19.2	16.0	6.8
$1.00 to $2.50 loss	26.2	20.8	18.3	29.2	21.2	18.6
0 to $1.00 loss	18.1	18.8	29.0	19.7	19.7	29.4
0 to $1.00 gain	11.9	15.6	23.9	10.2	15.1	23.9
$1.00 to $2.50 gain	16.2	14.7	14.0	14.6	14.5	13.8
More than $2.50 gain	9.0	13.8	7.9	7.0	13.5	7.6
Mean months elapsed from stop date to measure of wage loss	8.0	9.1	—	8.5	9.2	—
N	210	1,005	7,184	157	902	6,695

Note: The wage differential is calculated for each respondent as predicted wage minus actual wage. Thus the positive mean wage differentials represent a wage loss. See text for more details on these estimations. The Total Control Group columns include other job separations.

more likely than the control group to realize a wage gain of more than $1.00. But the displaced are much *less* likely to have a wage differential near zero (that is, between plus $1.00 and minus $1.00) and are nearly twice as likely to realize a wage loss exceeding $1.00.

Table 2–6 continues the investigation of the wage profiles of the displaced by reporting on the difference between predicted and actual wages at survey period $t + 3$. The results are rather surprising. On average more than 27 months after displacement the wage trajectories of these respondents continue to show a wage loss approaching 60 cents for all those displaced and nearly 72 cents for the displaced who were not in construction at the time of displacement. These are nearly identical to the corresponding wage loss figures computed at period $t + 1$. Thus, although even at $t + 1$ the wage loss associated with displacement is relatively modest, it is also apparently enduring for this sample of workers. This finding is consistent with the literature emphasizing the importance of career streams and suggests that the consequences of a career disruption even for these young workers cannot be readily overcome.

Comparing the distributions of the wage differentials for the displaced and control groups sheds further light on this conclusion. Both groups are about equally likely to realize a wage gain greater than $1.00 and are about equally likely to experience a wage loss of under $2.50. But the displaced are considerably less likely to show a small positive wage gain and much more likely to show a severe wage loss of over $2.50. This comparison points to the existence of a subset of about one-quarter of the displaced who suffer a severe and possibly very enduring wage erosion.

The Determinants of Wage Loss or Gain

Tables 2–5 and 2–6 show considerable variance in departure from the predicted wage trajectory at both periods $t + 1$ and $t + 3$, with some workers even showing an appreciable wage gain following displacement. Understanding why some workers gain and others lose is important both from a policy standpoint and for understanding the rigidities imposed on career development by labor market structures. A priori one might expect that few factors would be predictors of postdisplacement wage differentials consistently over the time span covered by these data and across the variety of contexts in which displacement has occurred. For example, whether blue-collar or white-collar workers fare better following displacement likely depends on whether the displacement occurred in the late 1960s or late 1970s and what alternate job opportunities were common in the local labor market. In short, it makes sense to ask not what explains greater wage loss or gain following displacement but under what circumstances does a certain sort of worker fare better or worse.

Table 2–6
Wage Differential in Period $t + 3$ Following Displacement and Other Job Separations, Including and Excluding Construction

	Including Construction			Excluding Construction		
	Displacements	Other Job Separations	Total Control Group	Displacements	Other Job Separations	Total Control Group
Mean wage differential in cents at $t + 3$	58.9	19.2	0.0	71.7	16.8	1.6
Percentage losing or gaining						
$2.50 or more loss	22.7	17.3	9.9	24.4	17.3	10.0
$1.00 to $2.50 loss	23.1	23.1	21.9	22.6	22.7	22.0
0 to $1.00 loss	19.0	18.1	23.1	20.8	18.3	23.4
0 to $1.00 gain	10.2	14.5	18.8	9.5	15.0	19.1
$1.00 to $2.50 gain	13.9	10.9	14.7	12.5	10.5	14.5
More than $2.50 gain	11.1	16.2	11.5	10.1	16.2	11.1
Mean months elapsed from stop date to measure of wage loss	27.1	29.4	—	27.9	29.5	—
N	216	947	6,441	168	851	6,008

Note: The wage differential is calculated for each respondent as predicted wage minus actual wage. Thus the positive mean wage differentials represent a wage loss. See text for more details on these estimations. The Total Control Group columns include other job separations.

Unfortunately, the small number of displaced workers at hand cannot support the number of interactions implied by the latter question. We must content ourselves with investigating the broader question of whether any factors stand out as being consistent predictors of the differential between predicted and actual wages across the variety of contexts covered by these data. A number of factors suggest themselves as being potentially important. These are

1. *Tenure with period* t *employer.* Those who have been with the same employer from which they were displaced for a number of years are more likely to have invested in firm-specific and nontransferable skills and to have seen their general human capital atrophy. Additionally, because these workers have not had to find a new job any time in the recent past, they should be less informed about alternate job opportunities and hence should have a harder time finding a new job. Finally, seniority provisions of employment contracts often entitle long-tenured workers to wage bonuses and other benefits which cannot easily be replaced if the employment relationship is severed. For these reasons, tenure with the pre-displacement employer should be associated with a larger wage differential upon reemployment, although the young age of these workers may attenuate a tenure effect here.

2. *Age.* In general older workers are assumed to be less adaptable, less mobile and hence less available to take advantage of alternative opportunities, and less desirable to new employers who must invest in their workers' training. Thus, age should be associated with a larger wage differential. However, this effect may be attenuated here given the narrow age range of this sample.

3. *Employment in construction.* Severance of an employment relationship should be less severe; in fact, severance is often routine for those in craft labor markets, for whom occupational identification is paramount. Those in construction should thus suffer least from displacement.

4. *Alternative employment opportunities.* Those displaced from an industry, occupation, or region in general decline will have few alternative employment opportunities that can make use of their available skills. Such workers should be the most likely to suffer upon displacement.

5. *Race.* Black workers suffer the additional handicap of racial discrimination in trying to adjust to displacement. Note that this is different from asking whether blacks have different wage growth profiles than whites, a question adequately addressed elsewhere (Rosenfeld, 1980) and effectively netted out here by having included race in the wage growth prediction equations. Instead we ask whether blacks who suffer displacement depart significantly more from their projected wage trajectory than do whites who suffer displacement.

6. *Family responsibilities.* Displaced workers who are compelled by family obligations to procure immediate reemployment may not have the luxury of prolonged job search. Their reemployment wages may suffer accordingly.

7. *Other factors related to skill specificity.* It has been speculated that both blue-collar workers and the less well educated may be more adversely affected by displacement because their skills are less transferable across employers.

8. *Predisplacement wages.* Net of education, those with higher predisplacement wages should have a harder time finding reemployment at comparable wages. This difficulty arises because such workers were initially employed at a rate exceeding their marginal productivity or credential level, or because their higher-than-average wages represent a return for skills learned on the job and hence at least partly nontransferable. For these reasons, those with higher predisplacement wages should fare worse upon reemployment, other things equal.

In testing these hypotheses we use as a dependent variable the difference between the respondent's predicted wage at period $t + 1$ or $t + 3$ and his actual wage at these time points. A wage loss occurs if the predicted wage (assuming no displacement) exceeds the actual wage which occurs following displacement. A regression equation relates this wage differential (predicted wage minus actual wage) to characteristics of each young man and the community in which he lives. A positive coefficient for any one characteristic means that the likelihood of a wage loss is greater as this variable increases in size. For example, a positive coefficient for the wage rate means that as a young man's wage rate grows, he is more likely to experience a wage loss following displacement.

The measures of independent variables are as follows: number of months worked for employer before displacement (*Tenure*); age in years (*Age*); three dummy variables for whether the respondent's predisplacement job was in the construction, manufacturing, or service industry, respectively (the omitted category, all other industries, to which construction, manufacturing, and service industries are compared); a dummy variable for race, coded 1 if black, 0 if not (*Black*); three dummy variables for whether the respondent was displaced from a professional/managerial, clerical/sales, or craft occupation (semiskilled or unskilled blue-collar occupations make up the category to which other occupations are compared); years of education (*Education*); number of dependents as a measure of family responsibilities (*Dependents*); predisplacement hourly wages in cents, measured at time t and adjusted to 1981 dollars (*Wage at* t); and six measures of alternate employment opportunities in the respondent's local labor market and occupational specialty. Three of these six are dummy variables for whether the respondent changed his occupation (*Changed Occupation*), industry (*Changed Industry*), or place of residence (*Changed Residence*). The first two of these utilize the Census three-digit codes in survey t and $t + 1$ or $t + 3$ in determining whether a change occurred and all three are coded such that 1 means a change occurred, and 0 means there was no change. Our prior expectation is that a change in one or more of these attachments is indicative of the respondent's difficulty in finding reemployment in the same locale or in a similar kind of work and thus reflects declining labor market opportunities. All three should have positive coefficients since for these changes a wage loss would be more likely. A change of occupation or industry should have a positive coefficient partly because the respondent is forced to forsake previous occupation-specific or industry-specific investments in human capital. The final three measures of alternate employment opportunities are a dummy for whether the respondent lived in an urban community at the time of displacement (*SMSA Residence*); the average annual growth rate of the respondent's industry during a 5-year period spanning his date of displacement[8] (*Industry Growth*); and the annual unemployment rate of the respondent's local labor market, based on CPS figures, with one implied decimal (*Unemployment Rate*). The first two of these are expected to have negative coefficients and the final one a positive coefficient since we expect wage losses to be lower in urban communities with high growth rates and higher in communities with high unemployment rates. Finally, to crudely control for cost of living differences associated with a geographic move to a low-wage area, a dummy variable is included for whether the respondent lived in the non-South before displacement but lived in the South when postdisplacement wage was measured (*Moved to the South*).[9]

Before presenting these results we remind the reader of several reasons militating against our finding very large effects. First, in Mick's (1975) judgment the effects of displacement are fairly indiscriminant; white- and blue-collar workers of both races, of all education levels, and from all locales suffer severely from an employment disruption. No one is immune from its effects, nor are any set of characteristics a guarantee of an easy transition to reemployment. Second, we argued above that the determinants of the wage differential are likely highly contingent upon the context in which the displacement occurred. With a sample size too small to support the interactions, this judgment implies that many of the more interesting effects may be lost. Finally, the wage differential variable treated as dependent is measured with substantial error, as the only modestly high R-squareds in the wage equations for the nondisplaced samples insures. Although regression coefficients are themselves unaffected by well-behaved measurement error in the dependent variable, higher standard errors will be one notable consequence of the greater error variance. Accordingly, some sizable coefficients may fail to attain statistical significance at conventional levels.

Table 2–7
Regression Analysis of Predicted Wage Minus Actual Wage at $t + 1$ and $t + 3$ for Displaced Workers

| | Wage Loss at | | | |
| | $t + 1$ | | $t + 3$ | |
	b	B	b	B
Independent variables				
Education	−9.09	−.065	9.73	.066
Tenure (in months)	−.212	.020	1.60*	.192
Months since displacement	2.69	.050	−.026	−.001
Age	−18.34**	−.200	−1.17	−.014
Black	134.76**	.203	−21.69	−.038
Dependents	−34.81*	−.146	−9.92	−.049
Unemployment rate	−1.03	−.082	.544	.055
Changed occupation	−64.84	−.099	76.32	.130
Changed industry	116.51*	.172	75.38	.119
Changed residence	127.75*	.140	−24.68	−.029
Industry growth rate	−887.51	−.107	525.6	.073
SMSA residence	41.91	.062	18.82	.031
Was in construction	74.09	.097	−52.75	−.072
Was in manufacturing	169.38*	.268	−62.02	−.112
Was in service	132.08	.187	−43.04	−.071
Was a professional/manager	158.93*	.184	37.04	.043
Was a clerk/salesman	−112.30	−.101	40.36	.039
Was a craftsman	−109.86*	−.162	57.07	.095
Moved to the South	−292.90	−.104	−16.07	−.005
Hourly wage at t	.267**	.343	.033	.042
Constant	1199.3	—	−758.2	—
R^2		.303		.105
N		160		155

Note: See text for details on variable constructions. Those respondents displaced more than once have only their most recent displacement counted.

*Significant at the .10 level.
**Significant at the .05 level.

Table 2–7, then, reports the results of a regression of wage loss on the variables just described. Looking at the results with wage loss measured at $t + 1$ shows confirmation for some of our hypotheses. Most decisive support is uncovered for the importance of local labor market characteristics. The actual wage for displaced respondents who changed industry or residence and were then reemployed was lower than we would have predicted in the absence of displacement. If we can infer from this that those who changed industry or residence or both did so because of declining opportunities in their local labor markets, the importance of the context in which displacement occurs looms large. Workers who move may suffer a greater wage loss than those who do not, because their initial unfamiliarity with labor market opportunities in the new communities causes them to accept a job at wages below par. Those who change industry lose returns of whatever industry-specific skills they might have accumulated at their predisplacement position. Workers who suffer least from displacement are those who find a ready market for their skills elsewhere in their communities. The importance of a vigorous economic climate in the local community is further corroborated by the nearly significant coefficient of the industry growth variable.

Hourly wage at time t (the survey before displacement) is also strongly related to postdisplacement wage differentials. Those with higher wages were more likely to experience wage loss because they had either accumulated some nontransferable job skills or other wage bonuses or were perhaps simply being paid more than the average wage for a person with their credentials. For any of these reasons they cannot hope to do so well upon reemployment as would workers with lower wage rates.

Black workers suffer an additional handicap upon displacement. This finding is particularly interesting in light of the fact that their race was already taken into account in plotting their expected wage trajectories in the absence of displacement.

Age is also significant in this regression equation, but its effect runs counter to expectations. Within the restricted age range of this sample, older rather than younger workers apparently have an easier time finding comparable postdisplacement employment. Possibly very young workers who are displaced before having a chance to accumulate work experience or acquire work skills are less attractive to new employers.

Contrary to expectations, those with more dependents are less likely to suffer wage loss, perhaps because their family obligations compel them to maximize pecuniary payoffs upon reemployment. Also contrary to expectations, at least upper level white-collar workers are more rather than less likely to suffer wage loss, perhaps because of the difficulty displaced professional and managerial workers have in establishing footholds in new organizational hierarchies. Craft workers by contrast are less likely to suffer a wage loss, probably because this occupational dummy variable rather than the industry dummy construction proxies better for employment in a craft-internal labor market. Finally, those employed in manufacturing before displacement on average suffer a significantly greater wage loss.

Somewhat surprisingly, neither tenure nor months since displacement has any significant effects in this sample, perhaps in the former case because wage at time t measures nontransferable job skills or other seniority-related wage bonuses more directly, and in the latter case because the range of variation is rather modest.

One independent variable not in this equation but included in preliminary analyses not shown here was a dummy variable measuring whether the respondent suffered any unemployment in the period following displacement. As mentioned earlier in this chapter, imprecision in the measurement of this variable has precluded our using it more systematically. But displacement may be a fundamentally different experience—and may imply something drastically different for wage trajectories—depending on whether the job separation was followed by unemployment or not. Therefore, for exploratory purposes we incorporated in the regression just described a dummy variable for whether the data revealed any evidence of unemployment in the period between displacement and the next survey date. Creation of this variable shows that 59 percent of displacements were followed by some unemployment; because of gaps in the work history data in the NLS this figure can only be an understatement of the true extent of unemployment. Descriptive statistics show the mean wage differential was 29 cents for those with no evident unemployment and $1.02 for those with some unemployment who were reemployed by survey $t + 1$. Thus, those with no unemployment fare substantially better, but both groups experience notable wage losses. When this variable was incorporated in the regression equation, the coefficient was large and in the expected direction (namely, 72.9) but did not attain statistical significance, presumably because measurement error increases its standard error. These results are available upon request.

Returning to our previous discussion, we show in the second columns of table 2–7 the determinants of wage loss at time $t + 3$. Differences abound; few of the variables significant in the wage loss at $t + 1$ equation are significant here, and the regression coefficients are generally smaller in absolute value.[10] Apparently, circumstances causing early disadvantages in adjusting to displacement have relatively short-term effects, so that differentials between groups of displaced workers are quickly equalized. Note that this is not to say that the displaced have recovered from their employment disruption: the appreciable mean wage loss at time $t + 3$ as shown in table 2–6 belies that interpretation.

The one variable that is significant in the $t + 3$ equation is tenure as of the time of displacement. To some degree this result is predicated on our assuming that in the absence of displacement these workers would have maintained continued employment with their predisplacement employer, since their predicted wage equations imputed tenure at $t + 3$ equal to tenure at the time of displacement plus time elapsed since displacement. The significant effect of tenure should be interpreted in this light.[11]

Determinants of Postdisplacement Unemployment

One problem endemic to the procedures for explaining time $t + 1$ wage loss in the previous section is that all those workers still unemployed at time $t + 1$

are excluded from the analysis because they have no data for postdisplacement actual wages.[12] This sample selection may bias the findings of the previous section to an unknown degree. Investigating the determinants of prolonged unemployment is of interest in its own right, in understanding the consequences of displacement, and in interpreting the results of the previous section.

The results of a probit analysis of unemployment at time $t + 1$ are presented in table 2–8. The dependent variable was coded 1 if the respondent was unemployed, and 0 if working.[13] The independent variables are as defined for the analysis of wage loss, except whether the respondent changed occupations and whether he changed industries are omitted because these variables are undefined for the unemployed respondents.

Table 2–8
Probit Analyses of the Probability of Unemployment at Survey
$t + 1$ for Displaced Workers
(N = 260)

	Maximum Likelihood Estimate	Standard Error
Independent variables		
Education	− .0040	.0490
Tenure (in months)	.0032	.0030
Months since displacement	− .0304	.0165
Age	.0469	.0302
Black	− .0715	.2086
Dependents	− .0018	.0689
Unemployment rate	.0031	.0035
Changed residence	− 1.1109[a]	.5222
Industry growth rate	2.6300	2.3545
SMSA residence	.4217[a]	.2114
Was in construction	− .3931	.3722
Was in manufacturing	− .1366	.3199
Was in service	.2859	.3488
Was a professional/manager	− .8042[a]	.3797
Was a clerk/salesman	− .5009	.3587
Was a craftsman	.0882	.2337
Moved to the South	.9708	.9211
Hourly wage at t	− .0006	.0003
Constant	1.1111	2.4811

Note: See text for definitions of variables.
[a]Indicates asymptotic t is greater than 2.0 in absolute value.

The analysis of unemployment shows that some variables with significant coefficients have effects just opposite those uncovered for wage differential at $t + 1$ in table 2–7. Specifically, those who changed residence or were professional/managerial employees are more likely to be employed in period $t + 1$. The one other significant effect, *SMSA Residence,* also runs counter to expectations, since those living in an SMSA, where alternate opportunities are presumably more prevalent, are more likely to be unemployed. *Predisplacement Hourly Wage* is negatively related to unemployment and just fails to attain significance.

Apparently, then, the factors that impel one to accept reemployment soon after displacement are also associated with one suffering an above-average wage loss. Workers who change residence following displacement do so presumably in pursuit of alternative job opportunities. They may be successful in finding a new job, but their unfamiliarity with a new labor market may make it difficult for them to find well-paying employment. Similarly, the easy transferability of managerial and professional skills across employers causes white-collar workers to be quickly reemployed, but, at least at the outset, minus the bonuses or commissions to which they had been accustomed. The pattern of effects in predisplacement hourly wage can be interpreted the same way. Net of education, those with a higher time t wage possess more on-the-job training, making them more attractive to other employers and hence boosting their probability of being reemployed soon after displacement. But at least some of these skills are nontransferable, causing them to suffer a greater wage loss. In short, the factors associated with a smoother postdisplacement experience are not straightforward and defy facile generalizations.

Conclusions

The results of this chapter in many ways corroborate what others have discovered; after displacement, workers can expect to encounter difficulty finding other employment and may only get reemployed at a job paying considerably less than their previous one. Examining the distribution of wage loss around the mean of 73 cents for nonconstruction displaced workers shows in fact considerable variability in how workers fare. Possibly half lose as much as $1.00 or more in hourly wage and one-quarter lose $2.50 or more. Moreover, there is no evidence that the mean wage erosion abates even 2 or more years after displacement. For some workers the costs of displacement are thus severe and enduring.

For others, displacement is not nearly so devastating in its consequences. A considerable number of workers, locked by inertia in predisplacement jobs which may undervalue their credentials or skills, reap considerable financial advantage from forced job separation. This is not to say that the psychic trauma associated with involuntary job loss does not exact a high price, but that displacement may be a prod leading to more remunerative career advancement. But at least economically it seems that many young workers are sufficiently adaptable and the labor market sufficiently accommodating to cause the costs associated with involuntary job loss to be slight or non-existent and transitory.

Understanding why some workers fare so much better following displacement than others is a problem that defies easy generalization for reasons mentioned throughout this chapter. But it appears that the location in which the displacement occurs is of prime importance. Workers who lose their jobs in the midst of a local labor market and industry in general decline can expect to fare much worse than others. Since even young workers, who are presumably most adaptable, can suffer significant and persistent costs in these cases, a well-conceived policy response seems in order.

Notes

1. It is possible that a displaced worker returned to the predisplacement employer but left again before a subsequent survey. Also, some workers do return to their previous employer beyond the three-survey limit used here. As far as could be determined in only 3 percent of the displacements identified did this occur. As a practical matter then, these separations are generally permanent.

2. One or more of the criteria used in the definition of displacement were unavailable for survey years 1966 and 1967, and whether the respondent returned to an employer by the third year could not be ascertained for those who left their 1980 or 1981 jobs. The survey years from 1968 to 1978 are 1968, 1969, 1970, 1971, 1973, 1975, 1976, and 1978.

3. About 91 percent left their time t employer for reasons they listed as voluntary and 9 percent left unvoluntarily.

4. Perhaps the simplest strategy would be simply to compare the wages of the displaced before and after displacement and label this difference, once figures are adjusted to constant dollars, as the wage loss (or gain). This method allows each worker to serve as his own control but would underestimate the true wage loss by ignoring the possibility that wage growth might have occurred in the absence of displacement. An alternate strategy would be to regress wages at some common end point (in our case 1980, the survey following the last displacement) for a cross-section of displaced and nondisplaced respondents on standard human capital variables and one or several variables measuring whether the respondent had been displaced and years elapsed since displacement. One could interpret these coefficients as measuring the wage loss associated with displacement and gauge whether or not these effects recede with the passage of time. There are several problems with this approach, but two loom as especially critical. First, one cannot readily differentiate between period effects and the effects the passage of time has on lessening the impact of displacement. Second, and practically speaking more critical, is the sober assessment that the small

number of displaced respondents over the entire period means that the effect of displacement for any single survey year would be based on an extremely few cases and hence should be highly unreliable.

A third method of estimating wage loss, also not pursued here, is a pooled cross-section design, in which wage $t + 1$ is regressed on wage at time t, control variables and a dummy variable for whether the respondent was displaced from time t to $t + 1$; this method would hold all respondents whether displaced or not as the units of analysis with each respondent counted as many times as he had valid t and $t + 1$ data, where t and $t + 1$ are consecutive survey years. This approach seems to overcome many of the disadvantages of the previous methods but still suffers from several major limitations of its own. Specifically, in the absence of a series of interaction terms that would greatly complicate the equation, a pooled cross-section approach assumes that the determinants of wage change are constant for all periods t and $t + 1$, that these determinants are constant for those displaced and not displaced between t and $t + 1$, and finally that the effect of displacement is constant across all these periods. All these assumptions seem untenable.

5. Recall that to be in the control group at survey t the respondent had to (1) be at least 20 years old, (2) not be enrolled in school in either survey years t or $t - 1$, (3) have at least 2 years' tenure with his employer at time $t + 1$ or at the time of separation for those who changed employers between t and $t + 1$, (4) be employed in the private sector at time t, and (5) not be displaced from t to $t + 1$ (that is, not have involuntarily separated for reason given as layoff or plant closing or, if involuntarily separated, have returned to this employer by period $t + 3$).

6. Several examples should illustrate this procedure. Assume two displaced workers were identified. One was displaced sometime between the 1968 and 1969 surveys and was displaced from the job he held on the 1968 survey date; the second was displaced from the job he held on the 1975 survey date sometime before the 1976 survey. After all wages are converted to constant dollars, four wage-growth equations are estimated using the control group of workers who were not displaced. These are (1) 1969 ($t + 1$) wages regressed on 1968 and 1967 wages plus other variables mentioned, using the control group of workers who were not displaced from 1968 to 1969, (2) 1971 ($t + 3$) wages regressed on 1968 and 1967 wages and the other variables, for the same sample, (3) 1976 ($t + 1$) wages regressed on 1975 and 1973 wages and other variables for the sample of workers not displaced between 1975 and 1976, and (4) 1978 ($t + 3$) wages regressed on 1975 and 1973 wages and other variables, for the same sample. For the worker displaced from his 1968 job, coefficients from equations (1) and (2) are used to estimate predicted wages for this respondent in periods $t + 1$ and $t + 3$, respectively; coefficients from equations (3) and (4) are used to estimate predicted wages for the person displaced in 1975. These prediction equations use the respondent's predisplacement years of education and residence and impute tenure as equal to tenure as of displacement plus time elapsed from displacement to $t + 1$ or $t + 3$. Predicted wages in periods $t + 1$ and $t + 3$ are then subtracted from actual wages to get a measure of the wage loss (or gain) due to displacement for each respondent. Since the procedure outlined effectively controls for period effects in wage growth, these estimates of wage loss can be aggregated regardless of the survey year the displacement occurred, to get an average wage loss in the $t + 1$ period and in the $t + 3$ periods.

7. A priori this seems like a sensible way of estimating wage loss. However, much hinges on these procedures' generating predicted wages equal to the actual wages these respondents would have realized had they not been displaced, *at least in the aggregate*. Obviously we cannot evaluate the tenability of this assumption directly, but we can do so indirectly. In particular, we use these procedures to predict wages for displaced workers in the survey just before displacement (period t) using $t - 1$ and $t - 2$ wages and appropriate measures of the other variables as independent variables and using coefficients generated from the equations generated from the control group. We then compare this predicted wage with the actual wage they received in period t. If displaced workers have a wage profile comparable to those in the control group the expected value of this residual would be zero. Carrying out these procedures and aggregating across survey years resulted in a mean difference between actual and predicted wage of under 5 cents for the 172 soon to be displaced respondents with valid data on relevant variables. As a further but related test we regressed survey t wages on $t - 1$ and $t - 2$ wages, other controls, and a dummy variable for whether the respondent was displaced in the period just subsequent to survey t. This was done separately for each year t. In no case did the displacement dummy even approach significance. We take this as confirmation of the legitimacy of this estimation procedure. If the difference between predicted and actual wage in the periods $t + 1$ and $t + 3$ subsequent to displacement are substantially different from zero we believe this can confidently be interpreted as a measure of wage loss or gain.

8. The number of employees in each three-digit industry is coded from County Business Patterns (U.S. Department of Commerce) for the years 1964, 1970, 1975, 1979. For respondents displaced between the 1968 and 1971 survey dates, the average annual growth rate from 1964 to 1970 is used. For those displaced from 1971 to 1976, the industry growth from 1970 to 1975 is used. Those displaced from 1976 to 1980 have the 1975 to 1979 period growth rate used.

9. Additional variables, including whether the respondent experienced any unemployment following displacement, the Rotter locus of control scale, size of the local labor market, and residence in the South at the time of displacement, were tried but omitted when they failed to show significant effects. Other variables including whether the respondent was a union member at the time of displacement would be interesting to incorporate in these equations, but the absence of complete data on these items precludes their use.

10. The smaller coefficients suggest that failure to find significant effects probably cannot be traced to the higher error variance of the $t + 3$ equations for the sample of nondisplaced workers.

11. Since most of the hypotheses raised relate more to explaining degree of wage loss rather than wage gain, the $t + 1$ and $t + 3$ wage differential equations were also rerun with all wage gains recoded to zero. Results changed very little with this recoding implemented.

12. The potential bias is more likely to be a problem for the $t + 1$ wage loss equation since at $t + 1$ 26 percent of the displaced sample are unemployed, whereas only 9 percent are unemployed at $t + 3$ (see table 2–4). The sample sizes shown in table 2–7 do not differ greatly across these equations because by $t + 3$ a number of displaced respondents have been lost due to attrition of the sample.

13. The 14 respondents out of the labor force at time $t + 1$ were excluded.

References

Becker, Gary. 1975. *Human Capital.* New York: Columbia University Press.

Bendick, Marc, and Judith Radlinski Devine. 1982. "Workers Dislocated by Economic Change: Do They Need Federal Employment and Training?" In *National Commission for Employment Policy, Seventh Annual Report.* Washington, D.C.: U.S. Government Printing Office.

Bluestone, Barry, and Bennett Harrison. 1982. *The Deindustrialization of America.* New York: Basic.

Congressional Budget Office. 1982. "Dislocated Workers: Issues and Federal Options." Washington, D.C.: Government Printing Office.

Doeringer, Peter, and Michael Piore. 1976. *Internal Labor Markets and Manpower Analysis.* Lexington, Mass.: Lexington Books.

Gordus, Jeanne P., Paul Jarley, and Louis Ferman. 1981. *Plant Closings and Economic Dislocation.* Kalamazoo, Mich.: Upjohn Institute.

Mick, Stephen. 1975. "Social and Personal Costs of Plant Shutdowns." *Industrial Relations 14* (May):203–208.

National Council on Employment Policy. 1983. "The Displaced Worker in America: An Overdue Policy Issue."

Parnes, Herbert, and Randall King. 1977. "Middle-aged Job Losers." *Industrial Gerontology 4* (Spring):77–95.

Rosenbaum, James. 1979. "Tournament Mobility: Career Patterns in a Corporation." *Administrative Science Quarterly 24* (June):220–240.

Rosenfeld, Rachel. 1980. "Race and Sex Differences in Career Dynamics." *American Sociological Review 45* (Aug.);583–609.

Schumpeter, Joseph. 1950. *Capitalism, Socialism, and Democracy.* New York: Harper.

Shapiro, David, and Steven Sandell. 1983. "Age Discrimination and Labor Market Problems of Displaced Older Male Workers." *National Commission for Employment Policy, Report Pr-83-10.*

Spilerman, Seymour. 1977. "Careers, Labor Market Structure, and Socioeconomic Achievement." *American Journal of Sociology 83* (Nov.):551–593.

Stern, James.1972. "Consequences of Plant Closure." *Journal of Human Resources 7* (Winter):3–25.

U.S. Department of Commerce. 1965, 1971, 1976, 1980. *County Business Patterns, 1964, 1970, 1975 and 1979.* Washington, D.C.: U.S. Government Printing Office.

3
Adjusting to Recession: Labor Market Dynamics in the Construction, Automobile, and Steel Industries

David Shapiro
Stephen M. Hills

Many would designate 1973 as a benchmark year in the U.S. economy (for example, Lawrence, 1984). The oil price shock in that year sent a strong signal to American consumers that smaller, more fuel-efficient cars were desirable, and the subsequent shift to imported cars caused serious employment problems for American automobile workers. The automobile industry, in turn, had a serious effect on the steel industry, compounded by the fact that many foreign countries had built large modern steel facilities. The sharp competition from foreign steel led to numerous plant closures in the United States and highly publicized problems for specific communities which had depended heavily on the industry for an economic base. Finally, interest rates rose sharply after 1973, creating serious problems for the U.S. construction industry.

In this study we examine the decisions of young men who were employed in the U.S. automobile, steel, and construction industries in the early 1970s. We track their work experience through a deep recessionary period and compare it with the experience of men employed in other industries. We ask how rates of mobility differed from one industry to another and how mobility affected the rate of growth in earnings. We measure the degree of support that employees in these three industries received from unemployment insurance and compare it with the support received by workers employed in other industries. Finally, we examine the factors most responsible for interindustry mobility. Holding these factors constant, we ask what remaining differences in mobility existed across industries for young men in the early 1970s. Longitudinal data help to isolate the determinants of interindustry mobility for workers who did not return to the industries they left due to recession.

Because data for this study are available only through 1981, we cannot analyze the full labor market adjustment which occurred during the 1981–82 recession. We can, however, track workers through the mid-1970s, when the economy also went into a sharp recession, then recovered. After 1973, the employment and earnings of young men peaked, fell sharply, and by 1978 returned to prerecession levels. Adjustment to the 1975 recession was one of the most difficult since World War II, so these data may be assumed to carry important implications for the 1982 period as well.

Trends and the Business Cycle: Employment over the Past Three Decades, the 1975 Recession, and the Labor Market

Figure 3–1 provides an overview of private employment in selected sectors of the U.S. economy during the past 30 years.[1] Over the course of the three decades, employment in both durable and nondurable goods manufacturing grew only very modestly, and in the automobile and steel industries employment actually declined. Construction industry employment, by contrast, grew by nearly 50 percent over the same period, and other private sector employment more than doubled.

In addition to these divergent trends, differences by industry in the sensitivity of employment to the business cycle are also readily apparent in figure 3–1. Recessions and recoveries sharply influenced employment levels in durable goods manufacturing—especially in automobiles and steel—and in construction. The effects on employment in nondurable goods manufacturing were much milder, and elsewhere in the private sector the principal effect of a recession was to halt temporarily the secular growth in employment.

In terms of unemployment, the 1981–82 recession was the most severe economic downturn since World War II. Its predecessor, the recession of 1975, was the second most severe: the national unemployment rate averaged 8.5 percent during the year, and seasonally adjusted unemployment rates at midyear exceeded 20 percent in construction and reached 12 percent in manufacturing.

Total private sector employment, which was 2 percent higher in 1974 than in 1973, fell by 3 percent in 1975. By 1976 total employment in the private sector had regained its 1974 level, and employment growth continued through the remainder of the 1970s. In construction and manufacturing, employment declined from 1974 to 1975 and then increased in 1976 and beyond; but the magnitude of the decline was substantially greater in these two cyclically sensitive industries than in the private sector as a whole, and the pace at which employment recovered was considerably slower.

Figure 3–2 shows annual average industry employment indexes for 1973 onward for the same sectors of the economy depicted in figure 3–1.[2] Employment levels in 1975 in the cyclically sensitive industries were roughly 10 to 20 percent below their prerecession peaks, and these peaks were not reached again until 1978. Most hard hit by the recession was employment in automobile manufacture and in construction.

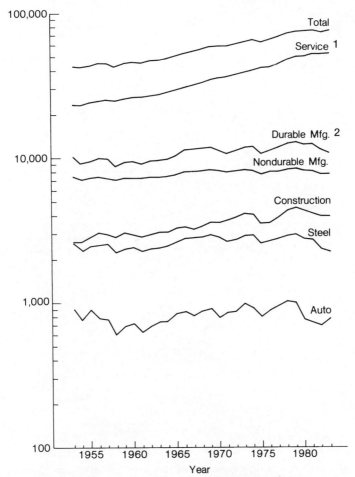

Source: *Employment and Training Report of the President* and *Monthly Labor Review*.

Note: The vertical axis constitutes a logarithmic scale. Intermediate categories between 100 and 1,000 are in hundreds, and between 1,000 and 10,000 in thousands, and between 10,000 and 100,000 in tens of thousands. The slope of each line represents changes in employment over time.

[1] All industries other than construction and manufacturing.

[2] Including automobile and steel industries.

Figure 3–1. Growth in Private Sector Employment by Industry, 1953–73

Rates of Interindustry Mobility as Shown by NLS Data

Male respondents to the National Longitudinal Surveys (NLS) of Labor Market Experience age 21–31 in 1973 demonstrated considerable interindustry mobility over a 5-year period, in part due to their youthful ages but

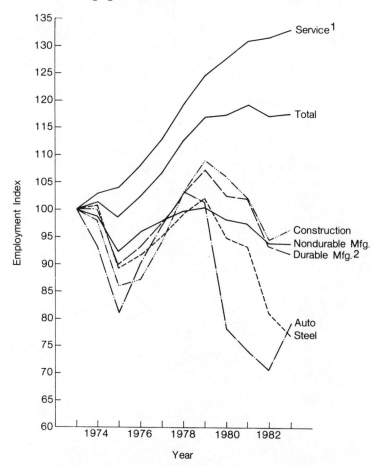

Source: *Employment and Training Report of the President* and *Monthly Labor Review*.

[1] All industries other than construction and manufacturing.

[2] Including automobile and steel industries.

Figure 3–2. Private Sector Employment Indexes by Industry, 1973–83
  (1973 = 100)

also due to the adverse economic conditions they faced. Only 60 percent of workers employed in construction or in automobile and steel industries were still employed in those industries in 1978. In contrast, 65 percent of young men remained in the nondurable goods sector, and 84 percent stayed in "other industries"—that is, the service sector, broadly defined[3] (table 3–1). Although these figures suggest that interindustry mobility was greatest for the industries hardest hit by the recession, the result may simply reflect the widely varying sizes of the sectors for which mobility was calculated.[4]

To obtain more accurate comparisons of interindustry mobility, we recalculated interindustry mobility for all two-digit industries, using the Standard Industrial Classification (SIC). Rates of change for all two-digit industries were averaged for the broader industry groups used in our analysis (table 3–2). We differentiated between men who left a two-digit industry temporarily and returned by 1978 (*returners*),[5] men employed in a given two-digit industry in 1973 but not in 1978 (*leavers*), and those who remained in the same industry for each of the interviews between 1973 and 1978 (*stayers*).

The mobility rate out of the construction industry was almost 40 percent, and the rate for the automobile and steel industries combined averaged 52 percent. The highest mobility rates, however, were in the category of "other durable manufacturing," where rates averaged 58 percent. In the service sector, the mobility rate exceeded that for the construction industry by about 5 percentage points, but nondurable goods manufacturing showed rates approximately the same as in construction. Thus durable goods manufacturing other than automobiles and steel had the highest mobility rates, automobile and steel intermediate rates, and the service, construction, and nondurable goods manufacturing industries the lowest.

Across all industries, a substantial proportion of young men were employed in another industry and then returned to the same two-digit industry in which they had been employed in 1973. Since we did not have a full work history to examine between 1973 and 1978, the actual rates of return mobility were undoubtedly higher than we calculated; nevertheless, the rates ranged from about 8 percent in the service sector to approximately 12 percent in the construction, automobile, and steel industries.

The service, nondurable manufacturing, and construction industries were virtually identical in terms of the proportion of young men who remained in the industry at every interview from 1973 to 1978. Nevertheless, construction and manufacturing had higher rates of return mobility than service. Once dislodged from any one of the two-digit service industries, young men were more apt to leave and not to return.

Stayers, Leavers, and Returners: Interindustry Mobility

Why do young men leave one industry for another? In recessionary periods, one answer to this question is obvious: some industries are harder hit by an economic downturn than others and thus jobs are reduced sharply. But even in recessionary periods many young men change industries voluntarily. The current debate over industrial policy makes it important to determine which factors influence their choices.

Table 3–1
Industry Group in 1978 by Industry Group in 1973

Industry Group, 1973	Percentage of 1973 Total	Percentage Distribution of 1973 Industry Group in 1978					
		Construction	Automobiles, Steel	Other Durable Goods, Manufacturing	Nondurable Goods, Manufacturing	Other Industries (Service)[a]	Total
Construction	12.8	59.5	1.9	4.8	2.5	31.3	100.0
Automobiles, Steel	8.9	5.7	59.2	15.3	3.3	16.5	100.0
Other Durable Goods, Manufacturing	16.6	5.5	6.7	55.3	6.1	26.4	100.0
Nondurable Goods, Manufacturing	12.8	2.7	2.6	5.3	64.5	24.9	100.0
Other Industries (Service)	49.0	4.5	1.6	4.6	4.9	84.4	100.0
Total	100.0						
Percentage of 1978 total		11.6	7.7	14.1	12.3	54.3	100.0

Note: Universe consisted of respondents employed in the nonagricultural private sector in 1973 who were interviewed and employed in 1978. Percentages are based on weighted data.

[a]Includes data for respondents who were in agriculture, mining, or the public sector in 1978.

Table 3-2
Mobility Patterns, 1973-78, by Industry Group in 1973[a]

Industry Group, 1973	Percentage Distribution of 1973 Industry Group			
	Stayer[b]	Leaver[c]	Returner[d]	Total
Construction	48.8	39.4	11.8	100.0
Automobiles, Steel[e]	35.9	52.4	11.7	100.0
Other Durable Goods, Manufacturing[f]	32.7	58.3	9.0	100.0
Nondurable Goods, Manufacturing[g]	47.9	41.2	10.9	100.0
Other Industries (Service)[h]	47.2	45.0	7.8	100.0
Total	44.1	46.6	9.3	100.0

Note: Universe consisted of respondents employed in the nonagricultural private sector in 1973 who were interviewed and employed in 1978. Percentages are based on weighted data.

[a]The mobility rates in this table do not directly correspond with the rates in table 3-1. Here mobility rates are calculated from one 2-digit industry to another. The rates are then averaged across the broad industry groupings shown. In table 3-1 the rates are calculated from one broad industry group to another.

[b]Stayer identifies respondents whose two-digit SIC industry did not change between 1973 and 1978.

[c]Leaver identifies respondents who left the two-digit SIC industry in which they were employed in 1973, and had not returned to that industry by 1978.

[d]Returner identifies respondents who left the two-digit SIC industry in which they were employed in 1973, but who had returned to and remained in the industry as of 1978.

[e]Includes motor vehicles and motor vehicle equipment, primary metal industries, and fabricated metal products.

[f]Includes lumber and wood products; furniture and fixtures; stone, clay, and glass products; machinery, except electrical; electrical machinery, equipment and supplies; other machinery; other transportation equipment; professional and photographic equipment and watches; and miscellaneous manufacturing.

[g]Includes food, textiles, apparel, printing, chemicals, and other nondurable goods.

[h]Includes transportation, communication and other public utilities, wholesale and retail trade, finance, insurance and real estate, business and repair services, personal services, entertainment and recreation, professional and related services.

Advocates of an active industrial policy for government claim that choices for jobs in various industries can and should be shaped by changing individual incentives to choose one industry over another. But industrial policy advocates are sharply divided about *how* incentives should be changed. Some believe market forces impose unreasonably high costs on individuals when they are forced to change industries too quickly (Bluestone and Harrison, 1982). This school of thought advocates policies to slow the shift of workers from declining to growing industries, as exemplified by protectionist tariff policies, generous transfer payments, and strong public support for collective bargaining. Others, on the other hand, advocate promobility policies which encourage shifts away from declining industries to new high-growth industries (Thurow, 1980); they emphasize economic growth and the benefits it confers on society as a whole. Both schools of thought, however, need information on the determinants of interindustry mobility, and the behavior of NLS respondents over the course of the business cycle can help cast light on this issue.

Mobility across industries can be either voluntary or involuntary. Voluntary mobility is regarded here as a form of investment behavior. That is, voluntary mobility should take place when workers calculate that the expected net advantage to changing industries is positive. From an investment perspective, the expected net advantage to changing industry equals the present value of the expected earnings stream in the new industry minus the present value of the expected earnings stream in the initial industry, minus the costs of moving from one industry to another.[6] Other things equal, then, factors that alter the expected net advantage to changing industries should also alter the likelihood of voluntary interindustry mobility.

Age should be inversely related to the propensity to change industry, ceteris paribus, since older workers have less time to recoup returns on investments in mobility. Tenure should also be inversely related to the likelihood of voluntary mobility. Greater job tenure (net of age or total work experience) results in higher earnings due to the accumulation of firm-specific training.[7] Individuals with greater job tenure (in 1973) will have higher expected earnings in an initial industry, but their long tenure will not necessarily influence expected earnings in an alternative industry, since the skills they acquire through tenure may not be transferable to the new industry. Thus less voluntary mobility should occur for workers with greater levels of job tenure. Characteristics of the industry in which a worker is employed will also influence the likelihood of interindustry mobility. Because earnings are higher, other things equal, in more heavily unionized industries, unionization should inhibit voluntary mobility.[8]

The larger the labor market within which an individual resides, the easier it will be for the individual to change industry without changing residence. The consequent lower cost of mobility suggests that, ceteris paribus, mobility will be greater in larger labor markets. Finally, evidence from the migration literature indicates that better educated individuals may be more efficient at acquiring and processing information (see, for example, Schwartz, 1973); hence, we expect schooling to be positively associated with voluntary mobility, other things equal.

Involuntary mobility consists primarily of layoffs. Nevertheless, workers who claim to have quit a job voluntarily may have done so because of poor economic conditions. From a human capital perspective, fixed costs of employment and firm-specific human capital are key influences on the likelihood that a worker will be laid off or quit in anticipation of a layoff.[9] In periods of slack demand, firms have an incentive to lay off employees. However, because firms make fixed-cost investments in the hiring (recruitment and screening) and training of their employees,[10] a firm experiences capital losses when laid-off employees do not return when recalled. Since laid-off workers may not return, the firm will try to lay off workers who are relatively cheap and easy to replace: workers with limited amounts of firm-specific training and those for whom hiring costs are low.

Because of the cost to employers of firm-specific training, seniority with a firm (job tenure) is expected to be inversely related to the probability that a worker will be laid off. Similarly, Oi (1962) presented evidence indicating that hiring and training costs rise (both absolutely and relatively) with worker skill levels. This finding suggests that involuntary mobility is less likely to be manifested by more highly skilled workers.

In addition to the individual characteristics, the characteristics of the industry that the worker is in will also influence the likelihood of involuntary mobility. Since industries are affected differentially by recession, mobility should be greater in industries where the impact of the recession is felt most.

To take account of the recession's effects on employment opportunities, we control for the rate of decline in employment by two-digit industry from 1973 until the trough of the recession.[11] In addition, to control for various other industry characteristics, we introduce a series of dummy variables for the broad industry groups shown in table 3–2. Once the differential effect of the recession on employment in each industry is controlled, we can then determine what additional effect broad industry classifications have on the probabilities of staying, leaving, or returning to an industry.

The data in table 3–2 reveal distinct differences in mobility patterns by broad industry group. These differences may simply reflect interindustry differences in factors such as age, tenure, or union status, or they may reflect unmeasured characteristics of industries. The analyses below include estimates of the determinants of mobility both with and without controls for broad industry groups, in order to ascertain the extent to which we can directly account for the differences in mobility patterns evident in table 3–2.

Table 3–3 reports coefficients of estimated ordinary least squares (OLS) equations[12] predicting the probability of leaving an industry. As anticipated, the rate of decline in employment throughout the initial phase of the business cycle was significantly related to the probability of leaving an industry and not returning. Holding constant variation in declining demand across industries, several other variables were also strongly significant. For each additional year of tenure in a firm, a young man was initially about 8 percentage points less likely to shift industries, but the effect of tenure diminished as tenure accumulated.[13] The size of the coefficient implies that tenure is an

Table 3-3
OLS Regression Analysis of the Determinants of Leaving 1973 Industry[a]

Independent variables	(1) Coefficient	(1) t	(2) Coefficient	(2) t	(3) Coefficient	(3) t
Education	.0061	1.03	.0058	0.98	.0068	1.16
Job tenure (in years)	−.079**	−7.50	−.088**	−8.38	−.091**	−8.56
Job tenure squared	.0043**	4.40	.0047**	4.85	.0047**	4.88
Age	−.00088	0.21	.0020	0.47	.0018	0.44
Professional	−.088*	−2.00	−.098*	−2.24	−.085+	−1.94
Managerial	−.087*	−2.05	−.080+	−1.90	−.057	−1.36
Craft	−.081**	−2.69	−.045	−1.44	−.047	−1.52
Employment fall[b]	−.0036+	−1.73	−.0002	−0.09	—	—
Union[c]	−.0017**	−2.72	−.0025**	−3.76	—	—
Labor force size (in 1,000s)	−.000	−0.99	−.000	−1.34	−.000	−1.27
Black	.034	1.05	.029	0.90	.029	0.91
Construction	—	—	−.247**	−5.25	−.247**	−5.24
Auto-steel	—	—	.047	0.97	.0068	0.14
Nondurable manufacturing	—	—	−.120**	−2.82	−.123**	−2.88
Other industries (service)	—	—	−.170**	−3.76	−.104**	−3.05
Constant	.625	4.71	.785	5.77	.629	4.83
R^2	.077		.102		.093	
F	12.23		12.09		12.65	
Sample size	1,617		1,617		1,617	

[a]Dependent variable equals 1 if respondent left the two-digit SIC industry in which he was employed in 1973 and had not returned to that industry by 1978; zero otherwise. All independent variables are measured as of 1973.

[b]The percentage change in employment between November 1973 and June 1975 in the two-digit SIC industry in which the respondent was employed in 1973.

[c]The percentage of production workers in the two-digit SIC industry in which the respondent was employed in 1973 whose wages were set by collective bargaining.

+ Significant at the .10 level, two-tailed *t*-test. *Significant at the .05 level, two-tailed *t*-test. **Significant at the .01 level, two-tailed *t*-test.

extremely important variable, particularly for advocates of a promobility policy. Retraining programs which are not targeted at those already unemployed (for instance, a voucher system or modification of the Individual Retirement Account to provide for retraining) would likely have an impact only on the vocational choices of workers with extremely short job tenure.[14]

All three variables that identify more highly skilled workers—*Professional, Managerial,* and *Craft*—are associated with a reduced probability of leaving one's industry. Workers who have relatively large amounts of training are 8–10 percentage points less likely to shift industries than are workers without such training. On the other hand, education has no effect on inter-industry mobility, other things equal. The education variable has the expected sign in the regression equation, but it is not statistically significant and its size is small. *Age,* unlike *Tenure,* likewise has little independent effect on mobility between industries, and blacks are no more or no less likely to shift industries than whites. Our hypothesis for the effects of labor market size on mobility was not supported by the regression equation.

American unions are often viewed as a major impediment to inter-industry mobility, and indeed a variable measuring the degree of collective bargaining coverage is highly significant in the regressions reported in table 3–3.[15] The estimated effect is nevertheless small. For each percentage point increase in an industry's collective bargaining coverage interindustry mobility declines by only 0.2 percentage points. Thus an increase in the fraction of an industry covered by collective bargaining from 50 percent to 100 percent would directly reduce the interindustry mobility of young men by only about 10 percentage points. Unionism may have an indirect effect on the rate of mobility, however, by increasing the job tenure of individual workers and thus reducing mobility. Previous research shows that unionism does reduce the quit rates of workers, although the effect is larger for older than for younger workers (Blau and Kahn, 1983).

Once individual differences and the cyclical sensitivity of industries are controlled, some industries may still differ from others in terms of mobility. In the second column of table 3–3 we tested for possible differences across industries by comparing each of four broad industry categories with *Other Durables,* durable manufacturing other than automobiles and steel. After controlling for the variables in our regression model the differences among broad industry groupings were very much more pronounced than appeared to be the case in table 3–2. Column 2 of table 3–3 shows that workers in non-durable manufacturing, the service sector, and construction were all considerably less likely to shift to other industries after the completion of a full business cycle, but for construction workers this was particularly true. When compared with workers in manufacturing, young construction workers were twice as likely to remain in their industry than were service workers or workers in nondurable manufacturing industries. This probably reflects the industry-specific skills that construction workers gain through on-the-job training and apprenticeship. On the other hand, automobile and steel workers did not differ significantly from workers in any of the other durable manufacturing industries as far as their mobility rates were concerned. We might have expected the automobile and steel industries to emerge as special cases, and indeed if the data had been drawn from the 1981–84 time period perhaps these industries would have demonstrated a much different adjustment process. But for the 1975 recession, at least, the automobile and steel industries were quite similar to other durable goods manufacturing industries.

Two variables are included in the regression equation to measure characteristics of the general environment in which work occurs within industries, namely the cyclical sensitivity of industries to recession-induced changes in employment, and the degree of collective bargaining coverage by industry. When broad industry dummy variables were entered in the equation, the first of these two variables was no longer significant, and when both variables were omitted from the equation (table 3–3, column 3), very little change occurred in the estimates for individual regression coefficients (with the exception of the coefficient for service industries, which became smaller in absolute value). Broad industry characteristics served just as well to predict interindustry mobility as did specific measures for the cyclical sensitivity of more narrowly defined two-digit industries.

The alternatives to leaving one's industry (as defined here) include both staying in the industry throughout the period from 1973 to 1978 and returning to the industry at some time during the period following a post-1973 departure. Equations which were estimated with *Stayer* as the dependent variable (not shown here) told virtually the same story as those in table 3–3. That is, workers with greater tenure in 1973 were more likely than those with less tenure to stay in their 1973 industries, but the marginal impact of tenure diminished as tenure increased; professional, managerial, and craft workers were significantly more likely than other workers to remain in their 1973 industries, other things equal; workers employed in industries particularly hard hit by the recession were less likely to remain; and those employed in more heavily unionized industries were more likely to stay in their 1973 industries. In addition, construction workers and those employed in non-durable goods manufacturing and in other industries were all significantly more likely than those in durable goods manufacturing to remain in their 1973 two-digit industry, ceteris paribus.

A parallel analysis was conducted to examine the determinants of returning to one's industry. This analysis also included a variable measuring the magnitude of the recovery in employment (between June 1975 and November 1978) in the two-digit industry in which an individual is employed. The variable had a positive coefficient, as anticipated, but it was not significant. In fact, no variable other than *Tenure* (with a positive coefficient) was significantly related to the probability of returning to one's 1973 industry; hence, no results for this analysis are reported here.

In addition to the results reported in table 3–3 and the parallel results for stayers, we also estimated comparable equations in which the dependent variables indicated mobility status as of 1981 instead of 1978. The purpose of these supplementary estimates was to test for the robustness of the results. By extending the period covered to 1981, we reduced the proportion of stayers and increased the proportion of leavers (and returners). This contributed to changes in the magnitudes of some of the coefficients (for example, the effects of tenure on inhibiting leaving and encouraging staying were slightly weaker when the period was lengthened to 8 years); but the general pattern of results in table 3–3 was substantially replicated in these supplementary equations.[16] Hence, the factors that help account for mobility behavior over the full business cycle were also relevant several years beyond.

We had anticipated that extension of the time frame to 1981 would reveal differences between the automobile and steel industries on the one hand and other durable goods manufacture on the other. More specifically, in view of the sharp declines in employment in automobiles and steel associated with the 1980 and 1981–82 recessions (see figure 3–2), we expected workers in the automobile and steel industry group to be significantly less likely than those in other durable goods manufacturing to still be in their 1973 industry as of 1981, and significantly more likely to have left their 1973 industry by 1981. These expectations were not borne out by the data.[17]

The Consequences of Recession: Joblessness

How individual workers fare during a recession varies considerably across industries. Here we ask how workers in cyclically sensitive industries compared with others during the 1975 recession, how well government policy offset the costs that workers incurred, and whether an analysis of the consequences of the recession would yield further insight into the movement of young men from one industry to the next.

In the 1975 recession young workers differed by industry in the incidence and duration of joblessness. They also differed in the proportion who received government assistance (unemployment compensation) and in how long the assistance lasted. The figures on the incidence of unemployment, in particular, show just how cyclically sensitive the construction, automobile, and steel industries proved to be when young male workers were followed throughout the entire recessionary period. Men who were employed in the service sector at the beginning of the recession showed a declining incidence of unemployment as the recession progressed and they grew older (table 3–4). In contrast the incidence of unemployment rose sharply in construction

Table 3-4
Unemployment Experience and Receipt of Unemployment Insurance by Industry Group in 1973, Selected Years, 1973-78

	Construction	Automobiles, Steel	Other Durable Goods, Manufacturing	Nondurable Goods, Manufacturing	Other Industries (Service)	Total
Percentage with some unemployment, last 12 months						
1973	29	19	16	13	15	17
1975	42	30	20	16	13	20
1976	28	24	16	9	10	14
1978	21	18	14	12	8	12
(Sample size)	(289)	(216)	(365)	(315)	(1,068)	(2,253)
Average annual weeks of unemployment (those unemployed)						
1973	10	10	11	14	10	11
1975	18	19	17	18	16	17
1976	15	18	16	18	17	17
1978	12	12	10	14	13	12
(Average sample size, all years)	(88)	(52)	(64)	(53)	(132)	(388)
Percentage receiving unemployment compensation (those unemployed)						
1973	31	36	35	47	28	33
1975	62	81	76	77	50	65
1976	62	58	54	48	40	51
1978	55	47	56	45	41	48
(Average sample size, all years)	(88)	(52)	(64)	(53)	(132)	(388)
Fraction of weeks unemployed which were compensated (those with some UI)						
1973	88	63	79	69	84	80
1975	83	93	86	75	82	81
1976	75	81	84	73	89	81
1978	87	84	82	81	77	82
(Average sample size, all years)	(45)	(30)	(35)	(29)	(52)	(191)

Note: Statistics are weighted to adjust for the oversampling of blacks.

and the automobile and steel industries. During 1975 the incidence of unemployment was more than twice as great in the automobile and steel industries than in the service industries and more than three times as great in construction. All manufacturing industries showed some cyclical sensitivity but
not nearly as much as the three industries central to this study. The incidence
of unemployment rose by about 25 percent in manufacturing from 1973 to
1975. Over the same time period, the incidence of unemployment increased
45 percent in construction and by 57 percent for young men who were initially employed in the automobile or steel industries.

To a degree, government policy compensated workers in cyclically sensitive industries more heavily than workers in the industries which were less
affected by the 1975 recession. Fifty percent of men in the service sector
(sectors were defined as of the beginning of the business cycle in 1973) who
experienced unemployment in 1975 received unemployment compensation,
but in construction the figure was 62 percent and in automobiles and steel a
very high 87 percent (table 3–4). Sharp changes also occurred over time in the
fraction of unemployed workers receiving unemployment insurance (UI). In
the automobile and steel industries the proportion of unemployed workers
receiving UI rose from 36 to 81 percent and then fell again to 47 percent. In
construction the changes were much less pronounced. Even though construction workers experienced the highest incidence of unemployment when the
recession was most severe, the rise in the fraction of unemployed construction
workers receiving UI was much less pronounced, from 31 percent to 62 and
then back to 55.

Changes in the proportion of men who were UI recipients probably
reflect differences across industries in patterns of eligibility for UI. The deep-
ening recession brought a higher incidence of involuntary unemployment,
especially in the manufacturing sector. As a result, more young men employed
in manufacturing would have been eligible to receive UI. The lower proportions of young men receiving UI in the service sector would therefore imply a
greater number of voluntary job changes in that sector, accompanied by some
unemployment. The relatively low proportions of unemployed men receiving
UI in the construction industry could reflect special restrictions on eligibility
which exclude workers with irregular income throughout the year.

Over time, UI recipients reported that a strikingly stable proportion of
their unemployment was compensated through UI (table 3–4) and the variation which did appear may be the result of small sample size. The fraction
was approximately 81 percent in each year from 1973 to 1978. The liberali-
zation of rules for providing extended unemployment benefits during the
1975 recession must have matched fairly well the more prolonged duration of
unemployment that these men experienced.

Both unemployment and the degree to which it was offset by government
policy could be important factors in determining who left or stayed in an

industry. In recessionary periods UI could help retain workers in an industry from which they might otherwise withdraw, thus protecting firm-specific skills which would be lost through recession induced mobility. Our data point to a relationship among the amount of unemployment, the degree to which the unemployment is offset through UI, and the individual's status as a stayer, leaver, or returner to a particular industry.

After dividing young men into two sectors of employment, we find that in both the manufacturing/construction sector and in the all-other-industry sector, the highest proportions of young men experiencing unemployment were among industry leavers (table 3–5). In manufacturing and construction, the highest proportions of unemployed workers who also received UI were among stayers and returners. The same was true for returners in all other industries. These data thus suggest that the government transfer payment policies are related to interindustry mobility. The sample sizes for returners are quite small, however, so conclusions must be tentative.

The Consequences of Recession: Wage Growth

A second consequence, both of recession and interindustry mobility, is a potential decline in wage growth. From beginning to end of a recessionary

Table 3–5
Unemployment and Receipt of Unemployment Insurance by Mobility Status and Sector of the Economy, 1975, 1976, and 1978[a]

	Manufacturing/Construction			All Other Industries		
	1975	1976	1978	1975	1976	1978
Percentage with unemployment in each year						
Stayers, 1973–78	24	16	13	4	5	6
Leavers, 1973–78	28	20	19	20	15	11
Returners, 1973–78	26	21	10	16	10	5
Total sample size	1,185	1,185	1,185	2,253	2,253	2,253
Of those with unemployment, the percentage receiving UI						
Stayers, 1973–78	75	71	67	46	34	33
Leavers, 1973–78	68	52	42	49	38	44
Returners, 1973–78	75	36	55[b]	68[b]	68[b]	54[b]
Sample size, those unemployed	339	236	206	151	116	97

[a]Statistics are weighted to adjust for the oversampling of blacks.

[b]Sample size less than 25. Returners were only 8 percent of the respondents in manufacturing and construction and 11 percent of the respondents in all other industries. Depending on the year and the sector of employment, returners ranged from 5 to 12 percent of the respondents who were unemployed.

period, different percentage changes in wages might be expected for typical young men who stay in a given industry, leave an industry for good, or leave and return. In part, different patterns of wage growth derive from variation in the amount of joblessness, which slows the accumulation of work experience and thus affects wages. More important, however, is the effect on wage growth of changing from one firm to another, because for virtually all workers, changing industry means changing firms as well. Wage rates are strongly influenced by tenure within a firm, and wages may grow less rapidly as workers shift from firm to firm, unless the skills learned in one firm are readily transferable to another. To measure the relationship between inter-industry mobility and wage growth, we hold constant age, education, and race, and examine the effect of joblessness and firm tenure on wage changes from 1973 to 1978. We rely heavily on Lazear's model for wage growth. Lazear's basic model (1976, pp. 549–550), adapted to conform to the circumstances of the sample being considered here,[18] yields a wage-growth equation where the natural logarithm of the hourly wage in 1978 minus the natural logarithm of the hourly wage in 1973 is a function of education, age, and the amount of time that a young man was without work.

Other things equal, wage growth is expected to be higher for persons with more schooling, reflecting evidence that more highly educated individuals engage more heavily in on-the-job training. Wage growth should be lower for older persons who have greater work experience as well as age and hence—given optimizing models of investment in on-the-job training (such as Ben-Porath, 1967)—have less incentive to invest in training at the margin. Finally, wage growth is expected to be lower for those experiencing joblessness because individuals who spend less time working are likely to acquire less on-the-job training, other things equal.

An important aspect of on-the-job training that is not explicitly taken into account in our wage growth equation is firm-specific training. Workers' investments in firm-specific training serve to increase their wages (Becker, 1975), so a worker's wage growth should depend on changes in his stock of firm-specific skills. Sandell and Shapiro (1978) have provided empirical evidence indicating that investment in firm-specific training increases with a worker's job tenure, and Bartel and Borjas (1977, 1981) have emphasized the importance of expected job tenure as a determinant of investment in firm-specific skills. Therefore, we modified Lazear's model to incorporate job tenure and firm-specific training in 1973 and 1978. Regression estimates for the model are shown in table 3–6, columns 1 and 2. Each of the coefficients from the model is statistically significant with the expected sign, although inclusion of the two tenure variables reduces the magnitude and level of significance of the variable measuring joblessness (*Time Not Employed*).[19] Before controlling for tenure, wage growth is significantly more rapid for blacks, but after tenure is controlled, the race variable is no longer statis-

Table 3–6
OLS Estimated Wage-Growth Equations, 1973–78[a]

	(1)		(2)	
	Coefficient	t	Coefficient	t
Independent variables				
Education, 1973	.016*	2.02	.016*	2.02
Age, 1973	−.014*	−2.38	−.014*	−2.30
Joblessness, 1973–78 (time not employed)	−.062**	−3.15	−.038+	−1.83
Tenure, 1978	—	—	.022**	4.28
Tenure, 1973	—	—	−.020*	−2.52
Black	.093*	2.05	0.71	1.57
Married	−.019	−0.48	−.023	−0.58
Constant	.278	1.59	.227	1.29
R^2		.021		.039
$\bar{R}^2$		.016		.032
F		4.35		5.78
Sample size		1,020		1,020

[a]Dependent variable equals the natural logarithm of the hourly wage rate in 1978 minus the natural logarithm of the hourly wage rate in 1973.

+ Significant at the .10 level, two-tailed *t*-test.

* Significant at the .05 level, two-tailed *t*-test.

** Significant at the .01 level, two-tailed *t*-test.

tically significant.[20] As is typically the case in wage-change equations (Bartel and Borjas, 1981; Corcoran, Duncan, and Ponza, 1983), only a small proportion of the variance in wage growth is accounted for by the explanatory variables.

The wage-growth equations show no explicit link between wage growth and the mobility status of workers. However, two variables in the equations are closely linked to mobility status: *Time Not Employed* between 1973 and 1978, and *Job Tenure* as of 1978. The amount of time not employed between 1973 and 1978 may constitute both a cause and a consequence of mobility status. That is, layoffs and unemployment may prompt some workers to seek jobs in new industries; even in the absence of layoffs or prior unemployment, a worker's decision to seek employment in a new industry may result in a period of job search while unemployed or simply a period of time not working.

The mean value of time not working for the full sample analyzed in table 3–6 is just over half a year. For those who remained in their 1973 industry up through 1978, time not working averaged 0.47 years, while the corresponding figure for those who left their 1973 industry and had not returned by 1978 was 0.77 years. Among returners, average time not employed between 1973 and 1978 was 0.52 years. Thus, *Time Not Employed* varies directly with mobility status; and in particular, the greater employment stability (lesser time not working) of stayers contributes to more rapid wage growth for them as compared to their more mobile counterparts.[21]

Job tenure as of 1978 also depends on mobility status. However, because tenure measures the duration of a person's attachment to a firm and mobility status is defined with respect to the two-digit industry in which the person works, lack of mobility does not always mean ever-increasing tenure. That is, those who change industries between 1973 and 1978 must have job tenure in 1978 of less than 5 years, but those who do not change industries may or may not have 5 or more years of tenure by 1978. Similarly, those who return to their initial firm may or may not have job tenure in excess of 5 years as of 1978. Overall, the mean values of 1978 job tenure for stayers, leavers, and returners equal 7.1, 3.2, and 5.0 years, respectively. If 1978 tenure has a positive impact on wage growth, stayers should experience more rapid growth in earnings than either leavers or returners.

Taking into account both time not employed and subsequent job tenure, then, the means presented imply that, other things equal, wage growth should be greatest for stayers and smallest for leavers, with returners experiencing wage growth more nearly like that of stayers. More specifically, the coefficients of the second equation in table 3–6 in conjunction with the means of time not working and 1978 tenure by mobility status yield the following implications: a married white male age 25 in 1973 with 13 years of schooling and 3 years of tenure in 1973 would be expected to experience wage growth of about 14 percent as a "typical" stayer, while the corresponding figures for leavers and returners would be about 4 percent and 9 percent, respectively. Overall, our results are quite consistent with the findings of Borjas (1981), who, in considering job mobility and earnings, concludes that nonmobile workers tend to achieve significantly higher wages over the long run.[22,23]

Workers in various industry groupings should also experience different rates of wage growth across the business cycle, stemming from differences in mean values for *Job Tenure* in 1978 and for *Joblessness* from 1973 to 1978. These differences in mean values, in turn, reflect the proportions of young men by industry who stay in, leave, or return to the industries in which they were employed as of 1973. Table 3–7 shows mean values for *Job Tenure* as of 1978 and for *Joblessness* across the same broad industry groupings we have used throughout this chapter. In column 3 are shown the predicted values for wage growth based on the estimated regression equation reported in table 3–6, column 2. Again, the predicted values are calculated for white males age 25 in 1973 with 13 years of schooling and 3 years of tenure in 1973. For these "typical" respondents, wage growth in construction was by

Table 3–7

Joblessness, Job Tenure, and Predicted Values for Wage Growth of Typical[a] Male Respondents, by Industrial Sector, 1973–78

	Mean Value Time Not Employed	*Mean Value Tenure 1978*	*Predicted Wage Growth*
Construction	0.55	2.7	.041
Automobiles, Steel	0.61	7.2	.137
Other Durable Goods, Manufacturing	0.57	5.9	.110
Nondurable Goods, Manufacturing	0.63	5.8	.105
Other Industries (Service)	0.71	4.6	.096

[a] *Typical* defined as 25-year-old white males with 13 years of schooling and 3 years of job tenure in 1973.

far the lowest, with a predicted value of about 4 percent. The low rate of growth stems mostly from the high rate of interfirm mobility among construction workers. Mean job tenure was only 2.7 years in 1978 compared with 7 years in automobile and steel industries and 6 in other durable goods manufacturing. Predicted wage growth for automobile and steel industries and for other durable goods manufacturing were correspondingly high—13.7 percent in the former and 11 percent in the latter. Construction and the automobile and steel industries were exceptional in their low and high estimated rates of wage growth. In all other sectors of the economy young men averaged 10 to 11 percent growth rates.

Conclusions

A combination of forces is set in motion during a deep recession. Long-term trends in adjustment to the market are heightened, and individuals are forced to consider what their long-term prospects may be in a particular industry when joblessness rises dramatically. On the other hand, long-term trends and recessionary changes in employment are not identical. State and federal policymakers should not confuse recessionary conditions with the long-term health of key industries.

We distinguished here between cyclical changes and other long-term shifts from industry to industry in two ways. First, we followed respondents through time, making use of the longitudinal data to determine who stayed consistently in an industry throughout the recessionary period, who left and then returned by the end of the period, and who left and did not return.

We then compared young men who left and did not return with all others. Second, when analyzing interindustry mobility we controlled for the decline (or less rapid growth) in employment across industries during the recessionary period. Holding constant the cyclical sensitivity of industries, we asked what other factors were related to the interindustry mobility of young men. The number of years spent in a given firm or organization was strongly related to mobility, but neither age nor education had significant effects. More highly skilled workers and those employed in highly unionized industries were less mobile. The degree of unionization, though statistically significant, did not translate into a strong numerical impact on mobility. Unionism's strongest effect may be indirect by increasing the tenure that a young man attains with a given firm and thus reducing the probability of interindustry mobility.

Even after controlling for recessionary-induced shifts in employment across two-digit industries, the broad distinctions we drew between sectors of the U.S. economy were highly significant. In fact, when variables describing broad industrial sectors were entered into a regression equation, differences in the rate of growth or decline in employment by two-digit industry were no longer significant determinants of interindustry mobility. For young men we found no difference in interindustry mobility between the automobile and steel industries and all other durable manufacturing industries, despite the special attention that has been placed on these industries in recent years. Even when we extended our analysis to 1981, young men employed in automobile and steel manufacture in 1973 were no more likely to leave those industries than young men employed in all other durable manufacturing industries. All else constant, nondurable manufacturing was quite similar to the broadly defined service sector in terms of interindustry mobility. The probability of leaving these sectors was 12 to 15 percentage points less than in durable goods manufacturing. Construction workers were the most strongly attached to their industry. Mobility rates out of construction were 24 percentage points less than in durable goods manufacturing.

Descriptive data on the impact of the 1975 recession showed the unevenness of effects across industries. In construction, the proportion of young men experiencing some unemployment throughout the year rose from 29 percent in 1973 to 42 percent in 1975. In the automobile and steel industries the fraction rose from 19 percent to 30 percent. Industries other than manufacturing and construction, however, showed *no* rise in the proportion of young men unemployed at some time throughout the year.

We found some relationship between a young man's receipt of unemployment insurance and his mobility status subsequent to the 1975 recession. In industries other than construction or manufacturing returners were more likely to receive unemployment insurance than either stayers or leavers. In manufacturing and construction, stayers were more likely to receive UI, followed by returners and leavers. These patterns undoubtedly reflect the larger proportions of voluntary quits among leavers.

Perhaps more interesting was the proportion of unemployment compensated among those who did receive UI. In each year from 1973–78, about four-fifths of the total weeks of unemployment that our respondents experienced were ones in which UI was received. Thus, on average, about 20 percent of the unemployment that UI recipients experienced in the 1975 recession was uncompensated. Because this proportion was stable throughout the recession, we conclude that extended UI benefit provisions must have matched fairly well the more prolonged durations of unemployment these men experienced when the recession was at its most severe point.

Finally we examined the relationship between the business cycle, interindustry mobility, and growth in wages between 1973 and 1978. Other factors constant, we predicted that a "typical" young man who stayed consistently in a particular industry would have experienced a 14 percent growth in wages from 1973 to 1978. Wages of a similar young man who left his industry of employment in 1973 and returned would have grown by 9 percent. Very little of the difference in rates of growth between men who stayed in an industry and men who left and returned was due to the greater joblessness of the returners. Rather, shorter firm tenure when they returned accounted for most of the difference, implying that even after returning to an industry, many young men had jobs with different firms. We predicted that men who left an industry and did not return in 1978 experienced wage growth of only 4 percent over the cycle, other factors constant. Only 1.5 percentage points of the 11-point difference between men who stayed and men who left industries by the recession's end was due to the greater joblessness of leavers. Thus, even for very young men, the net result of interindustry mobility is a significant short-run decrease in the growth of wages. Our analysis did not address long-run changes in wage rates.

The short-run costs to mobility were also apparent when examining the predicted rates of wage growth in various industries. Construction, the industry to which young workers were most strongly attached, nevertheless showed the lowest wage growth. Lower than average tenure with any given firm was the source of the modest wage growth of about 4 percent. In contrast, "typical" young men in the automobile and steel industries showed a high rate of wage growth, almost 14 percent, despite the severity of the 1975 recession. This result may help to explain why the automobile and steel industries were not significantly different from other durable goods manufacturing industries in terms of the proportions of young workers who shifted industries during the recession. At least during the early 1970s, the prospects of relatively strong wage growth may have encouraged men who otherwise might have changed industries to wait for recall.

Notes

1. The use of a logarithmic vertical scale in figure 3–1 facilitates comparisons of trends and fluctuations across industries, because slopes are equivalent to percentage changes.

2. More precisely, "automobiles" represents "motor vehicles and equipment," "steel" represents "primary metal industries" plus "fabricated metal products," and "service" equals "total private sector" minus the sum of "construction" and "manufacturing."

3. Agriculture and mining were excluded from the sample of men employed in 1973, and because of sample size limitations, automobiles and steel were combined into a single category.

4. That is, for example, "automobiles, steel" includes only two two-digit SIC industries, while "other industries" includes several one-digit SIC industries. The broader the industry grouping the less interindustry mobility there will be. Hence, had we combined "automobiles, steel" with "other durables" into a single "durables" category, we would have found 66 percent retention in durables; had we aggregated up to all manufacturing, we would have found 72 percent retention between 1973 and 1978. For a listing of specific two-digit industries, which are contained in each of our broad groupings, see the notes for table 3–2.

5. The returners group does not fully account for all young men who may have left an industry briefly and then returned. The 1976 interview accounts for all jobs between 1975 and 1976 but the 1975 and 1978 interviews only record the respondent's current or last job. Thus between 1973 and 1975 or between 1976 and 1978 some mobility out of an industry and back in again could occur and not be reported. These cases are presently defined as stayers.

6. This formulation emphasizes the pecuniary motivation for mobility. A more complete treatment would also incorporate nonpecuniary considerations.

7. For a discussion of this point, see Sandell and Shapiro (1978, pp. 104–109).

8. Unions also influence nonwage aspects of employment so as to inhibit worker mobility.

9. For the formal model underlying our approach here to layoffs, as well as empirical applications to aggregate data on layoffs for three-digit manufacturing industries, see Parsons (1972).

10. The seminal work on fixed costs of employment is Oi (1962).

11. November 1973 corresponds roughly to when respondents were interviewed in 1973. Examination of seasonally adjusted monthly data on total nonagricultural employment revealed that the trough of employment during the recession was hit in June of 1975. Hence, the variable *Employment Fall* measures the severity of the recession in terms of employment.

12. Logit results are similar to those obtained using OLS.

13. The marginal impact of tenure on the probability of leaving one's industry is given by $\partial Leave / \partial Tenure = -.079 + .0086$ *Tenure*. This impact is negative for values of tenure up to approximately 9.2 years. At the sample mean of tenure (2.7 years), an additional year of tenure reduces the likelihood of leaving one's industry by more than 5 percentage points.

14. We tested for an interactive effect between a worker's job tenure and the magnitude of the decline in employment in the worker's industry, but failed to find evidence of any such effect.

15. Data on *Union* were obtained (and in some cases derived) from data presented in Freeman and Medoff (1979, tables 2.2 and 2.9, pp. 151–161 and 173).

16. One variable that was not significant in table 3–3 but is consistently significant (with the "wrong" sign) in the supplementary equations is labor force size. Conversely, there is no longer (as of 1981) evidence of a significant differential between workers in durable and nondurable goods manufacturing with respect to the probability of leaving (the coefficient is reduced by half), although the differential between the two groups with respect to the probability of staying remains and is virtually unchanged.

17. Had data been available through 1982, during which steel employment dropped precipitously and auto employment continued to decline, we might have found evidence to support our hypothesis.

18. Equation (2) corresponds to equation (8) of Lazear (1976, p. 550), with two modifications: reflecting the fact that our sample is considerably older than Lazear's, we have omitted his term measuring additional schooling acquired during the period, since such a variable would equal zero for nearly all of our sample; and we have also omitted a measure of total work experience as of the outset of the period. Since we use potential experience (*Age-Education-6*) as a proxy for total work experience, it is not possible to include all three variables (age, schooling, and experience) in the wage-growth equation simultaneously.

19. Joblessness is constructed based on information on weeks worked during three years of the 5-year period: 1974–76 and 1977–78. The total number of weeks worked during those 3 years was divided by 52 and then multiplied by 5/3 to give an estimate for the full 5-year period. The implicit assumption—that weeks worked during the 2 years for which data are not available are comparable to those for the 3 years for which data are available—undoubtedly introduces some measurement error into the variable, and thus its coefficient in the earnings growth equations will likely be biased toward zero.

20. The equations reported in table 3–7 include variables identifying blacks and respondents who were married with spouse present in 1973. Lazear found blacks to have significantly faster wage growth, while married men had significantly slower wage growth, other things equal. We included these additional variables to test for the presence of such differences.

21. The differences in time not employed by mobility status that are reported above are gross differences. In order to ascertain, at least roughly, the magnitude of these differences net of other factors, time not employed was regressed on age, schooling, marital status, race, tenure, and mobility status. The discussion of the preceding paragraph in the text implies that the coefficients of mobility status in this equation will suffer from simultaneity bias; but we felt that the results would nonetheless be interesting as an indication of rough orders of magnitude. Other things equal, time not employed was significantly greater for blacks and significantly smaller for older, better educated, and married individuals, as well as for those with greater tenure in 1973. Net of these figures, leavers averaged 0.3 years more time not employed than stayers (the coefficient being highly significant), while returners averaged (a statistically insignificant) 0.1 years more than stayers.

22. As Borjas (1981) notes, and as indicated by the empirical work of Bartel and Borjas (1981), wage growth associated with job mobility is likely to depend substantially on whether the mobility is voluntary (in which case wages typically increase) or involuntary (in which case wages typically do not change or decline). Unfortunately, the data did not permit us to identify whether the mobility of leavers and returners was voluntary or involuntary.

23. In addition to the equations reported in table 3–6, we also estimated wage-growth equations that controlled for tenure in 1973 but not in 1978. The coefficient of the 1973 tenure variable was close to zero and not significant, indicating that it is the *change* in tenure that influences wage growth and not the initial level of tenure.

References

Bartel, Ann P., and George J. Borjas. 1977. "Specific Training and Its Effects on the Human Capital Investment Profile." *Southern Economic Journal 44* (no. 2, Oct.):333–341.

———. 1981. "Wage Growth and Job Turnover: An Empirical Analysis." In Sherwin Rosen, ed., *Studies in Labor Markets.* Chicago: University of Chicago Press for National Bureau of Economic Research.

Becker, Gary S. 1975. *Human Capital,* 2nd ed. New York: National Bureau of Economic Research.

Ben-Porath, Yoram. 1967. "The Production of Human Capital and the Life Cycle of Earnings." *Journal of Political Economy 75* (no. 4, Aug.):352–365.

Blau, Francine D., and Lawrence M. Kahn. 1983. "Unionism, Seniority and Turnover." *Industrial Relations 37* (no. 3, April):331–345.

Bluestone, Barry, and Bennett Harrison. 1982. *The Deindustrialization of America.* New York: Basic.

Borjas, George J. 1981. "Job Mobility and Earnings over the Life Cycle." *Industrial and Labor Relations Review 34* (no. 3, April):365–376.

Corcoran, Mary, Greg J. Duncan, and Michael Ponza. 1983. "A Longitudinal Analysis of White Women's Wages." *Journal of Human Resources 18* (no. 4, Fall): 497–520.

Freeman, Richard B., and James L. Medoff. 1979. "New Estimates of Private Sector Unionism in the United States." *Industrial and Labor Relations Review 32* (no. 2, Jan):143–174.

Lawrence, Robert Z. 1984. *Can America Compete?* Washington, D.C.: Brookings Institution.

Lazear, Edward. 1976. "Age, Experience, and Wage Growth." *American Economic Review 66* (no. 4, Sept.):548–558.

Oi, Walter. 1962. "Labor as a Quasi-Fixed Factor of Production." *Journal of Political Economy 70* (no. 4, Oct.):538–555.

Parsons, Donald O. 1972. "Specific Human Capital: An Application to Quit Rates and Layoff Rates." *Journal of Political Economy 80* (no. 5, Nov./Dec.):1120–1143.

Sandell, Steven H., and David Shapiro. 1978. "The Theory of Human Capital and the Earnings of Women: A Reexamination of the Evidence." *Journal of Human Resources 13* (no. 1, Winter):103–117.

Schwartz, Aba. 1973. "Interpreting the Effect of Distance on Migration." *Journal of Political Economy 81* (no. 5, Sept./Oct.):1153–1169.

Thurow, Lester. 1980. *The Zero Sum Society.* New York: Basic.

U.S. Department of Labor, Bureau of Labor Statistics. 1973–75. *Employment and Earnings.* Nov. 1973 to June 1975.

———. 1973–83. *Monthly Labor Review.*

4
Adjusting to the Structure of Jobs: Geographic Mobility

Stephen M. Hills

C hanges in the locational structure of jobs in the U.S. economy have caused researchers to place increased emphasis on the ability of workers to adjust to the market through geographic mobility. U.S. society is highly mobile, both in terms of the jobs that individuals hold and the choices that they make about geographic location. Nevertheless, the degree of mobility depends greatly on definition. A definition that treats geographic mobility together with decisions about job changes is necessary for measuring the responsiveness of the U.S. labor force to shifts in the distribution of jobs from one region to another.

Also changing in the United States is the distribution of paid work effort within individual households. The dramatic rise in the labor force participation of women means that decisions affecting employment no longer rest solely on the job prospects of men. Furthermore, when men lose jobs involuntarily, the employment of wives often is critical in determining whether families must move quickly to new locations in search of jobs or whether they can afford to wait for employment conditions to improve in specific labor markets. As a consequence, geographic mobility should also be studied as a joint decision-making process between husbands and wives.

Finally, a decision about geographic location may also be a joint decision between an employee and an employer. Company transfers often are required by large businesses and governmental organizations, but the degree to which the new job assignments are voluntary or involuntary has largely been ignored in the mobility literature.

Early mobility studies dealt with aggregate data, examining the determinants of net and gross migration flows (for example, Greenwood, 1969). Though useful for economic and social planning, such studies did not cast much light on the individual determinants of migration. Other studies have focused on the factors influencing individuals in their migration decisions (Lansing and Mueller, 1967; Greenwood's 1975 review; Polacheck and Horvath, 1977; Cebula, 1979; Black, 1983), but the microlevel data used in these analyses seldom link geographic mobility with job mobility. Exceptions to this generalization are the studies by DeVanzo (1976) and Bartel (1979).

Using National Longitudinal Surveys (NLS) of Labor Market Experience data from 1973, Bartel shows that for a number of key variables which help to determine migration, the link between geographic mobility and the set of conditions surrounding job mobility can be quite important. According to her analysis, migration consists of three separate probabilities: the probability of migrating and quitting, the probability of migrating and being laid off, and the probability of migrating and not changing employers (a company transfer).

Following Bartel, this study examines geographic mobility decisions as they are linked to decisions about employment. New data contained in the NLS 1981 survey of men age 29–39 permit us to distinguish between a geographic movement that accompanies a change of employer and a move that occurs even though a young man continues to work for the same employer in the same location. In yet a third case a geographic move occurs while a young man works for the same employer in a new location (a company transfer).

Moves that are not transfers are classified, in this study, according to whether they accompanied a voluntary or involuntary change of employer. Transfers are classified according to the expectations of employees and employers—that is, whether the move occurred largely because the employee wanted it or largely because the employer demanded it. Both moves and transfers are then compared with voluntary and involuntary job changes that occur without geographic mobility.

The data of concern in this chapter describe moves that occurred from 1976 to 1981, a period when joint decisions about geographic location, job changes, and the distribution of work between husbands and wives should be highly interrelated. In this period few of the moves that occurred will be related to postschooling or postmilitary decisions. The period from 1976 to 1981 is important also because the recession of 1975 undoubtedly had a special impact on the mobility decisions made subsequently by many of the respondents.

The Extent of Mobility

Young men were highly mobile in the period from 1976 to 1981, at least when data on their geographic movements are considered separately from data on employment. Thirty-four percent of the young men interviewed in 1981 were either in a different town or city than they had been in 1976 (30 percent), or despite being in the same city or town in both years, had lived percent), or despite being in the same city or town in both years, had lived elsewhere in the interim (4 percent). In Bartel's study 20 percent of NLS young men moved between 1971 and 1973 (Bartel, 1979, p. 776).

Figures on overall mobility can be misleading, however, for making inferences about the responsiveness of the labor force to changes in the structure of jobs. Only a portion of the moves that young men made between 1976 and 1981 involved decisions about both geographic location and employment. Only 11.5 percent of the men interviewed in 1981 had moved and changed employers in the 5 years prior to the interview. Another 4.7 percent moved and continued to work for the same employer but in a new location (that is, they were transferred). Half of the moves young men made between 1976 and 1981 did not involve, in other words, a decision about change in work site or employer. This finding emphasizes the importance of nonemployment-related reasons for geographic mobility, a fact increasingly recognized in research on geographic mobility (see, for example, Roseman, 1983).

Nonemployment reasons for moving may, of course, be important for men who changed jobs and changed employers, too. Table 4–1 reports the reasons for mobility across several different types of movers. Not surprisingly, employment-related reasons dominated the list for young men who were transferred. But even there, employment reasons were not the only ones for transferring. Contrary to the popular stereotype regarding intrafirm transfers, many were largely voluntary. Less than half of the transfers indicated that they moved mainly at the insistence of their employer. The rest of the young men who were transferred reported that the change was largely because they wanted it. Employment-related reasons for moving were men-

Table 4–1
Percentage of Total Sample Reporting Selected Reasons for Moving, by Type of Move, 1976–81[a]

	Type of Move				
Reason for Move	Same Employer, Same Location	Voluntary Change of Employer	Involuntary Change of Employer	Voluntary Transfer	Involuntary Transfer
Own employment	38.4	72.4	61.4	84.3	95.6
Wife's employment	2.4	1.2	2.4	—	—
Community	8.0	6.5	4.9	8.1	—
Family	33.1	18.3	21.6	10.4	—
Other unspecified	49.5	23.8	31.8	6.4	4.4
Sample size	569	123	247	84	53

[a]Multiple responses were allowed; thus, categories do not sum to 100.

tioned by almost 100 percent of those whose transfers were involuntary but by 84 percent of those transferred voluntarily. Family considerations were the most important other reasons for transferring voluntarily.

The reasons for moving also differed between those young men who involuntarily left their previous jobs and those who left voluntarily. Table 4–1 shows that among those who quit jobs voluntarily, the respondent's own employment was a more important reason for moving than it was for those who were laid off or unemployed immediately prior to moving. Why this difference occurs is unclear since the only other category in which the two groups significantly diverge was "other unspecified reason for moving."

The group in which family and other reasons predominated was, not surprisingly, the movers who shifted locations in a single labor market but continued to work for the same employer in the same location (column 1 of table 4–1). Though the data do not specify the reasons precisely, the decision to purchase housing rather than rent would undoubtedly be important. This study focuses on the movers reported in columns 2–5 of the table, all of whom changed work sites or employers and who expressed strong employment-related motivations for moving.

The Determinants of Geographic Mobility

As Bartel stresses in her study, a complex set of relationships exists among factors leading people to move from one location to another, depending on the type of job shift accompanying geographic mobility. I distinguish in the present analysis among six types of job and mobility status change:

1. A move accompanied by a voluntary change of employer
2. A move accompanied by an involuntary change of employer
3. A move accompanied by a voluntary transfer
4. A move accompanied by an involuntary transfer
5. No geographic move but a voluntary change of employer
6. No geographic move but an involuntary change of employer

The joint decision-making processes of husbands and wives and those of employers and employees are the focus of analysis for each of these groups.

The importance of wives' labor force participation on decisions to move depended, according to Bartel's study, on the conditions surrounding the move. Oddly enough, young men whose wives participated in the labor force were the most likely to be transferred, but a wife's labor force participation had little effect on the probability that a family would choose to move voluntarily. Wives' incomes also had restraining effects on the probability of transfer for the husband, but wives' incomes had little effect on the probability of a voluntary job change combined with moving or an involuntary job change combined with moving. These results raise questions about how husbands and wives decide whether or not to move, questions that can be resolved by analyzing data from a time period when more young men were married.

Regression Analysis of the Determinants of Geographic Mobility

Table 4–2 reports ordinary least squares (OLS) regression estimates for a set of equations used to predict the probability of falling into each of the six groups of movers and nonmovers I have identified. These regression equations were also estimated using maximum likelihood logit, and the pattern of results for significant coefficients was quite similar to that obtained using ordinary least squares. Only the OLS estimates are shown here, for ease of interpretation.

The independent variables associated with the six probabilities of moving and of changing jobs fall into three groups:

1. Characteristics of the respondent such as his education, work experience, health, and wage rate
2. Characteristics of the respondent's family that measure the way in which employment is shared with his wife, namely, his marital status, his wife's labor force participation, her income, and whether or not school age children belong to his household
3. Characteristics of the labor market environment in which decisions about employment and geographic mobility are made (the size of the local labor market, and its unemployment rate in the census year of 1970)

The results show much clearer patterns than those indicated in Bartel's study, and the addition of variables to control for race and for local labor market conditions also reveals new relationships. Bartel observed that the relationship between wage rates and geographic mobility was quite unclear unless one distinguished among the different types of moves that can occur, and my estimates greatly reinforce this conclusion. Wage rates are highly significant in all but one of the estimated equations, but the signs on the coefficients differ depending on the type of move. Low wages are significantly associated with a higher probability of moving for respondents who change employers, but for young men who transfer, high wages are associated with a higher probability of transfer. The degree of effect differs little between vol-

Table 4–2
OLS Regression Estimates of the Probabilities of Moving and/or Changing Jobs, 1976–81

| | Type of Move or Job Change | | | |
| | Leave Job Voluntarily and Move (1) | | Leave Job Involuntarily and Move (2) | |
	Coefficient	t	Coefficient	t
Independent variables				
Wage, 1976 (in dollars)	− .0056**	− 2.74	− .0046**	− 3.11
Black	− .0418***	− 3.45	− .0052	− 0.59
Poor health, 1976	.0135	0.77	.0107	0.84
Education, 1976	.0115***	4.95	.0022	1.29
Work experience 1976 (in years)	− .0002	− 0.14	− .0003	− 0.40
Married, 1976	− .0393***	− 2.81	− .0086	− 0.86
Presence of school-age children, 1976	− .0056	− 0.54	.0004	0.05
Wife participated in labor force, 1976	.0217	1.47	− .0019	− 0.18
Wife's income, 1976 (in 1,000s)	− .0019	− 1.02	− .00003	− 0.03
1970 size of labor force for residence, 1976 (in 100,000s)	− .0009*	− 1.91	.0002	0.51
1970 unemployment rate for residence, 1976	.0060**	2.13	− .0017	− 0.82
Respondent was unemployed, 1976	.0045	0.33	.0159	1.61
Constant	− .0444	− 1.13	.0428	1.51
R^2	.032		.008	
F	7.26		1.79	

*Significant at .10.
**Significant at .01.
***Significant at .001.

untary or involuntary employer changes. In each case a $1.00 increase in wage rates is associated with about a 0.5 percentage point decrease in the probability of migrating. In contrast, a $1.00 increase in wage rates is associated with an *increase* in the probability of transfer of between 0.2 and 0.4 percentage points.

The interrelationships between mobility and job changing are quite evident when the regression estimates for columns 1 and 2 are compared with those in columns 5 and 6. Men earning lower wages are signficantly more likely to be laid off and move than are those earning higher wages. This result does not stem, however, from the effect of wage rates on the probability of being laid off. Wage rates do not significantly influence the probability of

			Type of Move or Job Change				
Transfer Voluntarily (3)		*Transfer Involuntarily* (4)		*Leave Job Voluntarily and Not Move* (5)		*Leave Job Involuntarily and Not Move* (6)	
Coefficient	*t*	*Coefficient*	*t*	*Coefficient*	*t*	*Coefficient*	*t*
.0035***	2.66	.0020*	1.77	−.0103***	3.63	.0016	0.94
.0006	0.08	−.0116*	−1.77	−.0035	−0.21	.0037	0.37
−.0095	−0.85	.0014	0.14	−.0130	−0.53	−.0110	−0.73
.0034**	2.30	.0019	1.50	.0019	0.60	−.0113***	−5.85
−.0004	−0.60	−.0002	−0.29	−.0007	−0.45	−.0002	−0.17
.0144	1.62	−.0044	−0.58	.0377	1.95	−.0232**	−1.99
−.0057	−0.85	.0084	1.51	−.0210	−1.46	.0017	0.19
.0010	0.10	−.0072	−0.90	−.0235	−1.15	.0064	0.52
−.0006	−0.54	.0011	1.15	.0008	0.31	.0005	0.30
−.0002	−0.67	−.0003	−1.08	.0002	0.36	−.0008**	−2.04
.0005	0.27	.0023	1.49	.0018	0.45	.0015	0.64
−.0011	−0.12	−.0071	−0.96	.0215	1.13	.0233**	2.03
.0049*	−1.79	−.0228	−1.07	.1480***	2.72	.1938***	5.94
.012		.010		.008		.027	
2.72		2.19		1.74		6.15	

being laid off and not moving. Thus for young men who leave jobs involuntarily, earnings must be a key determinant in their decision to move or not. The relationship is not as clear for men who quit their jobs voluntarily, though. It is true that low wage men are more likely to quit a job and move (table 4–2, column 1), but wages are even more important in predicting who will quit a job and *not* move (table 4–2, column 5). Wages affect voluntary separations, then, but have little to do with the decision to move among those who quit their jobs voluntarily.

A strongly significant and positive relationship appears between years of education and the probability of a voluntary separation and move (table 4–2, column 1). Each year of education raises the probability by 1 percentage point, a result occurring despite an insignificant relationship between education and the probability of a voluntary separation and not moving (table 4–2, column 5). Thus education is an important factor in the decision to move, but it has little effect on the decision to quit a job. For men who were laid off, education was negatively related to losing a job: more highly educated men were less likely to be laid off. But education was positively related to being laid off and moving, though its statistical significance was weak. Together these results imply that more highly educated men were more likely to move, whether their job separation was voluntary or involuntary. More highly educated men were also more likely to be transferred regardless of whether the change was voluntary or involuntary (table 4–2, columns 3 and 4).

Interestingly enough, black workers were no more likely to quit and not move than were white workers once other factors were held constant (table 4–2, column 5), but they were significantly less likely than whites to quit and move (table 4–2, column 1). The size of the effect was large compared to other coefficients in the regression equation. Blacks were 4 percentage points less likely than whites to move after a voluntary job separation. Perhaps information about other communities and jobs is harder for blacks to obtain, especially if patterns of discrimination must be determined for each new community. Family and community ties may also be stronger for blacks than whites, thus inhibiting their mobility. Blacks do not differ from whites as far as involuntary job changes are concerned, however. The proportions who were laid off and moved, and who were laid off and did not move were the same for blacks and for whites (table 4–2, columns 2 and 6). Disproportionately fewer blacks than whites were transferred involuntarily, however, (table 4–2, column 4).

The change in the way work is shared between husbands and wives should presumably affect the mobility decisions that families make. We might expect families in which wives work to be less mobile and to become increasingly less mobile the more the wife earns. Both Bartel (1979) and DaVanzo (1976), however, have questioned this hypothesis. Bartel's study in particular finds a positive relationship between a wife's labor force participation and the probability of moving. The relationship derives, however, from equations predicting the probability of being transferred. It is hard to imagine why employers would be more inclined to transfer families in which both the husband and wife are employed. In fact, transfers should be more difficult under such circumstances.

Our estimates clearly do not support Bartel's finding. Married couples were less likely to move after a husband quit his job voluntarily (table 4–2, column 1). But neither a wife's labor force participation nor her income had a measurable effect in any of the regression equations reported in table 4–2. Only in equation (1) did wife's labor force participation approach statistical significance, but in the logit estimations wife's participation was consistently insignificant. The presence of school-age children did not inhibit mobility in any of the equations estimated.

If individuals respond to market signals as economic theory leads us to believe, geographic mobility should be sensitive to local labor market conditions. To test this relationship, I included variables in the regression equations that measure labor market size and the degree of unemployment in the local market. Conditions prevailing during the 1970 Census are used to proxy for long-run labor market conditions faced by respondents in their 1976 communities of residence. I expected more young men to move away from areas of high unemployment, regardless of the type of job separation and found that men who left jobs voluntarily did respond to high rates of unemployment by moving. Living in a community having a 1970 unemployment rate 1 percentage point higher than any other community's raised the probability of quitting and moving by 0.6 percentage points (table 4–2, column 1). For men who were laid off, conditions prevailing in the local labor market were not a significant factor in the decision to move. I also expected men who lived in larger labor markets to be less likely to move, and these men were indeed less likely to move following voluntary job separation (table 4–2, column 1).

In summary, young men do respond to market signals in the way that economic theory would suggest. Their wages are important determinants of moving, and young men respond to economic conditions in the local labor market. Their level of education is also an important determinant of mobility. Furthermore, economic explanations work better for mobility accompanying voluntary job separations than for mobility accompanying involuntary job separations. In the equation used to predict the probability of being laid off and moving, only the wage rate was significant. Nevertheless, for the education variable, the effect on the probability of layoff works in the opposite direction of the effect on moving, perhaps explaining the lack of significance for this variable in equation (2). How race affects mobility was further clarified by the equations. Blacks were significantly less likely than whites to move following a voluntary job change, and they were less likely than whites to be transferred involuntarily. Neither a wife's labor force participation nor her level of income affected mobility.

Transfers versus Movers

Literature on geographic mobility seldom distinguishes between employment-related moves and other moves, but even less attention is paid to the differences between moves resulting from company transfers and all other relocations. An advantage to working for a large corporate firm or for government is the ability to gather job information through the organization itself and to minimize the costs of changing jobs even when a geographic move is required. Yet little research has been done comparing the benefits of transfers with the benefits which occur from changing jobs either in a local job market or from one location to another.

A variety of outcome measures could be used to evaluate the role that company transfer policies play in the process of geographic mobility, but the focus here is on the stream of earnings that individuals expect in their current location, when compared with the stream of earnings they would expect after moving to a new location. Assuming that earnings are a primary motivation in moving, individuals should expect a steeper earnings profile over time if they move than if they do not.

Two theoretical traditions differ in their predictions about the stream of earnings which accompany company transfers, as compared with other types of moves. Standard economic theory, based on assumptions of competitive labor markets and rational economic behavior, predicts that an investment in job search should produce steeper wage profiles over time for those who invest time searching for new employment opportunities. Thus men who voluntarily change employers and their geographic location should recoup the costs of moving through the steeper wage profiles they expect to obtain.

The costs of search may differ significantly, depending on whether search occurs across organizations or within the communication channels of a single large organization. Because large organizations post jobs regularly and tend to give preference to internal job applicants, prospective job information should be less costly if obtained within the internal communication network of a large organization than if obtained across organizations. Therefore, men who transfer voluntarily will demand less steep wage profiles as inducements for changing jobs than will men who quit jobs voluntarily and move.

Voluntary transfers should receive higher postseparation earnings than involuntary transfers since a person who obtains a voluntary transfer will not accept the new position unless its benefits are at least as good as the old. The person who is transferred involuntarily, however, knows that the employer may in effect demote him by reducing his future chances for promotion if a transfer is not accepted. Thus, involuntary transfers should gain lower postseparation benefits than voluntary transfers, reflecting the discretionary power of the employer.

Men who are laid off should receive less benefit from their first postseparation job, all else constant, than men who quit. Those who quit should accept no less than the benefit received in their current job, as they build on their work experience to increase earnings. But men who are laid off may accept employment at a wage equal to or less than their current pay, reflecting the depreciation of firm-specific skills which often occurs with involuntary job loss.

According to the viewpoint just stated, the rank-ordering of job separations, when compared with those who neither separate from a job nor move is thus

1. Quit and move
2. Voluntary transfer
3. Involuntary transfer
4. Quit and no move
5. Layoff and move
6. Layoff and no move

This ranking assumes that the costs of changing geographic location are greater than the costs of changing firms. If the costs are equal, men who quit and do not move will be ranked the same as voluntary transfers (since transfers require that a person change geographic location). If, on average, the costs of changing firms exceed the costs of changing geographic location, men who quit and do not move will rank above voluntary transfers, but in all cases men who quit and move will be ranked first since they must cover both the costs of moving and of changing firms.

From a second viewpoint, the sociology of wage-determination is more important than economic decision making (Doeringer and Piore, 1971; Thurow, 1980). The presence of an organizational hierarchy makes it possible for men who transfer voluntarily or involuntarily to be compensated more generously after a move than men who change employers. Wages may be competitive at limited ports of entry to large organizations but be relatively divorced from the competitive market as an individual's tenure increases. Men who were employed initially by large organizations would gain larger benefits through promotion and transfer than men whose careers required them to change employers if transfers accompanied upward movement in the hierarchy of the organization. From this alternative viewpoint, men's earnings increases are more associated with organizational position and power than with their skills and work experience.

The rank-ordering of expected effects is different from that predicted by standard economic theory. Voluntary and involuntary transfers are expected to have the strongest relationship with increased earnings. Other types of job separation maintain the same relative rank-ordering since we assume that a job seeker, once outside the large organization, acts as predicted by competitive theory. The rank order becomes

1. Voluntary transfer
2. Involuntary transfer
3. Quit and move
4. Quit and no move
5. Layoff and move
6. Layoff and no move

To determine which viewpoint was most characteristic of the sample of male wage-earners, a wage-change equation was estimated, using as a dependent variable the slope of the earnings profile between 1976 and 1981 (ln 1981 wage rate − ln 1976 wage rate). Results are shown in table 4–3. The standard human capital variables of *Age, Education,* and *Job Tenure* were all strongly significant and in the direction that theory and previous studies would lead us to expect. Older, longer tenured employees showed less rapid wage growth, and higher wage growth was experienced by more highly educated workers. Blacks experienced less rapid wage growth than whites.

A series of dummy variables controlled for type of job separation, each compared with men who did not leave a job and did not move. The only significant variables were those controlling for job transfers. Men who transferred showed more rapid wage growth than men who did not. Men who quit their jobs voluntarily, however, showed no more rapid wage growth than men who experienced no job separations, were not transferred, and did not move. Variables which we expected to reflect choices based on economic motivations, namely moving and quitting a job voluntarily, were not significantly related to an improved wage profile. These results are consistent with the viewpoint that movement within the internal hierarchy of large organizations is the most important factor for ensuring steady wage growth over time. Since tenure was controlled in the wage-growth equation, we conclude that the improvement in earnings came from a young man's position in the hierarchy of his firm and not from his own work experience.

Distances Moved and Transferred

DaVanzo (1983) argues that distance proxies for the information costs of a move. If the arguments in the preceding section are true, then transfers and other moves should differ in terms of the distances moved. Longer distance moves may be more susceptible to failure, particularly if information must be obtained through the less reliable informal information channels of the marketplace or more formal information exchanges far removed from a young man's original location. Thus when distance moved is a dependent variable in a regression equation, a dummy variable for transfers relative to all other movers should have a positive sign. In other words, transfers move longer distances because they incur less costs in gathering information on moves.

Since the information argument regarding transfers applies to individuals and not to firms, however, differences should occur in the predictions for transfers which were voluntary and those which were largely initiated by the employer. Two dummy variables should therefore be included in the regression equation, only one of which (*Voluntary Transfers*) could be expected to have a positive sign.

Table 4–3
OLS Regression Analysis of the Outcomes of Geographic Mobility:
Percentage Changes in Wage Rates, Ln(Wage$_{81}$ − Wage$_{76}$)

	b	t
Independent variables		
Voluntary transfer	.084*	1.74
Involuntary transfer	.100*	1.71
Laid off and moved	.049	0.95
Quit and moved	.012	0.32
Laid off and no move	− .021	− 0.63
Quit and no move	− .006	− 0.29
No job separation and no move (base)	—	—
Age, 1976	− .011***	− 4.35
Black	− .031	− 1.67
Education (years)	.014***	4.65
Job tenure (years)	− .006***	− 2.83
Constant	.689***	8.31
R^2	.039	
F	9.14	
Sample size	2,238	

*Significant at .10.
***Significant at .001.

Finally, if migrants respond to the signals of depressed markets, we would expect unemployed migrants to be willing to incur higher costs in acquiring information for new and more favorable locations for work. To what extent this is true can be analyzed by contrasting the experiences of voluntary quits who moved with respondents who were laid off and then moved. I therefore included in the regression equation a dummy variable identifying involuntary separations among the men who moved.

Control variables in the regression equation were the same as those used to predict the outcomes of mobility, with the exception of one additional variable. I expected men who had friends and relatives in the location to which they moved to be willing to move longer distances, since friends and relatives should reduce the uncertainty involved in gaining information about new labor markets.

Results of the regression analysis were quite unsatisfactory (table 4–4). Virtually none of the independent variables entered into the regression equation were even close to statistical significance. Several explanations are possible for the poor results. The relationship between distance and the variables selected may be nonlinear. The costs of moving farther than a day's drive from the original location may be sharply different than the costs of staying

Table 4–4
OLS Regression Analysis of Distance Moved, Male Workers,
Aged 29–39 in 1981

	b	t
Independent variables		
Voluntary transfer	138	0.97
Involuntary transfer	39	0.24
Laid off and moved	88	0.73
Education	31	1.28
Work experience (in years)	8	0.77
Black	− 5	− 0.33
Friends and relatives	61	0.67
Occupation		
Professional managerial	− 157	− 1.23
Service	− 121	− 0.53
Blue collar (base)	—	—
Industry		
Agriculture, construction, and mining	129	0.83
Wholesale and retail trade	10	0.07
Government, transportation, and public utilities	− 55	− 0.38
Professional service, finance, insurance and real estate	− 159	− 1.13
Other service	− 77	− 0.43
Manufacturing (base)	—	—
Constant	1,920.48	—
R^2		0.30
F		0.67

within a day's drive, particularly if maintaining contact with friends and relatives is important. Also, the costs of moving versus not moving vastly overshadow any differential in costs which men incur moving short or long distances. Thus respondents may not differentiate between short and long distances once the decision to move has been made. Finally, we may simply know too little about the factors affecting the distances moved, thus incorporating in our model the wrong variables for predicting distance.

Conclusions

Distinguishing between voluntary and involuntary job changes and between transfers and nontransfers is important when studying both the determinants and the outcomes of geographic mobility. Young men and their families did respond rather directly to economic signals when making decisions whether or not to move. For men who quit their jobs voluntarily and then moved, the level of unemployment in their original location, the size of the local labor market, and their previous wage rate affected their decisions significantly. Blacks, however, were significantly less likely to move after quitting jobs voluntarily than were whites.

At the outset of this chapter several joint decision-making processes were hypothesized to affect the decision to move. The first, the joint process of leaving a job and moving was certainly important, since involuntary separations were quite different from voluntary separations. But the joint decision making of husbands and wives did not conform to expectations. It was hypothesized that if a man's wife participated in the labor force, the family would be less likely to move and that the probability of moving would diminish the more a wife earned. Neither effect could be found with the present data, and the positive relationship between a wife's labor force participation and geographic mobility reported previously by Bartel was likewise not confirmed by the data.

The joint decision-making process between employers and employees about mobility was clarified by this study. The stereotype that most intrafirm transfers are involuntary was not confirmed by the data. In fact, half of the transfers involving men in their 30s were voluntary. Some of the variables which affected voluntary transfers did not have any impact on involuntary transfers, but the most important difference was between all men who transferred and men who changed employers and moved. Men who had higher wage rates were more apt to be transferred, whereas men with lower wage rates were more apt to move and change employers. Thus if transfers were not distinguished from other types of movers, the effect of wage rates would not be nearly as strong as in the equations estimated.

Examination of the impact of various types of job separations on subsequent earnings led to the conclusion that the power that individuals in larger organizations exercise over wage rates may be more important than the power of the market. Only men who transferred from one work location to another showed an upward shift in their earnings profile when compared with men who did not change employers or geographic location. Other combinations of employer changes and changes in geographic location did not result in a significant increase in the rate of change in earnings.

It was hypothesized that the differences in the determinants of geographic mobility for various types of movers would also be reflected in the outcomes of mobility and in the distances that young men moved. This relationship did not appear to be the case. Variables which distinguished among various types of movers, when entered into regression equations predicting the outcomes of mobility, were highly insignificant. The modeling of outcomes overall was not terribly satisfactory, however. Perhaps better models of the outcomes of mobility will also prove to be sensitive to the distinctions among types of mobility.

References

Bartel, Ann. 1979. "The Migration Decision: What Role Does Job Mobility Play?" *American Economic Review* 69 (Dec.):775–786.

Black, Matthew. 1983. "Migration of Young Labor Force Entrants." *Socio-Economic Planning Sciences* 17 (no. 4):267–280.

Cebula, Richard J. 1979. *The Determinants of Human Migration.* Lexington, Mass.: Lexington Books.

DaVanzo, Julie. 1976. *Why Families Move: A Model of the Geographic Mobility of Married Couples.* Santa Monica, Calif.: Rand Corporation.

———. 1983. "Repeat Migration in the U.S.: Who Moves Back and Who Moves On?" *Review of Economics and Statistics* (May).

Doeringer, P., and M. Piore. 1971. *Internal Labor Markets and Manpower Analysis.* Lexington, Mass.: Lexington Books.

Greenwood, Michael. 1969. "An Analysis of the Determinants of Geographic Labor Mobility in the United States." *Review of Economics and Statistics* 51 (May): 189–194.

———. 1975. "Research on Internal Migration in the United States: A Survey." *Journal of Economic Literature* 13:397–433.

Lansing, John B., and Eva Mueller. 1967. *The Geographic Mobility of Labor.* Ann Arbor: Survey Research Center, University of Michigan.

Polachek, S., and F. Horvath. 1977. "A Life Cycle Approach to Migration Analysis of the Perspicacious Peregrinator." In R. Ehrenberg, ed., *Research in Labor Economics,* Vol. 1. Greenwich, Conn.: JAI Press.

Roseman, Curtis. 1983. "Labor Force Migration, Non-Labor Force Migration, and Non-Employment Reasons for Migration." *Socio-Economic Planning Sciences* 17 (no. 5):303–312.

Thurow, Lester. 1980. *The Zero Sum Society.* New York: Basic.

5
Household Costs of Unemployment

Lisa M. Lynch

The severity of the recent recession has generated a substantial amount of discussion on the link between unemployment and economic hardship. The emphasis of this discussion has changed over time for several reasons. With the increasing participation of women and young people and the expansion of government transfer payments, it has been argued that while unemployment may be increasing, its impact on a household's income has decreased. Such an argument assumes, however, that those households which experience unemployment have somehow been able to compensate for the income loss (typically of the primary breadwinner) with earnings from the spouse, children, and government transfers. The impact of unemployment on total annual family income will depend on three factors—the type of job lost and its associated wage rate, the amount of earnings that other family members can contribute, and income obtained from other sources, including unemployment compensation and other social welfare payments. Given that women and youths experience greater unemployment and when employed they have lower earnings, their ability to compensate for the loss of income of a primary earner may not be large. Second, although government transfer payments have expanded, higher unemployment rates are usually associated with increasing durations of unemployment, making it more difficult for households to replace income as they lose entitlement to benefits.

Many previous studies of the incidence and duration of unemployment have concentrated both theoretically and empirically on the determinants of the individual's unemployment experience rather than that of the household. Given the increasing percentage of households with multiple workers (in the 1981 National Longitudinal Surveys (NLS) of Labor Market Experience of young men, 65 percent of all married households had both respondent and spouse in the labor force), policymakers who analyze economic hardship using data only on individuals may draw the wrong conclusions. This chapter examines unemployment from a household perspective so as to study the impact on the labor market behavior of young men of the presence of other wage earners in the family. The theoretical model used is a standard job search model as described by Mortenson (1970) and Lippmann and McCall (1976). The question is whether a wife's labor market experience affects her husband's unemployment.

Characteristics of Households That Experience Unemployment

In the 1981 survey of young men aged 29–39, 80 percent of the weighted sample were married. Sixty-five percent of these households had more than one worker, and this percentage increased to almost 90 percent in black married households. Given the age of the cohort, I count as an additional worker only the spouse of the respondent, and I do not attempt to measure the spouse's "commitment" to the labor force.[1] Approximately 9 percent of young men who were in the labor force had experienced some unemployment during the survey year, but 16 percent of their households had had some unemployment during that year. Among these households experiencing unemployment, 58 percent had only the respondent unemployed, 32 percent had only the spouse unemployed, and only 10 percent had both the respondent and the spouse unemployed.

Typically, when policymakers examine the economic hardship of unemployment, they examine an *individual's* replacement ratio—the ratio of income *while unemployed* to expected net-of-tax income when employed. However, this ratio is not appropriate for evaluating the impact of unemployment on the household. Instead I have calculated the *household's annual income* replacement rate—that is, earned family income, unearned income, and all government transfer payments received over the survey year divided by the expected income if the respondent or his spouse or both had not incurred any unemployment during the survey year.[2] Table 5–1 reports characteristics of this replacement rate.

The results shown in table 5–1 seem to indicate that households with only the married or unmarried respondent working have greater difficulty than other households in replacing income over the year. Obviously, everything else equal, those households with two earners will have higher replacement rates. But in terms of the job search behavior of an unemployed individual, members of households with higher replacement rates may also have longer durations of unemployment. There does not appear to be any substantial difference in white and nonwhite households' ability to replace income lost due to unemployment. However, because blacks are disproportionately represented in the lower income categories, this finding does not suggest that black households experience the same economic hardship as white households in an absolute sense. Not surprisingly, it is clear that households which experience longer amounts of time unemployed are less successful in replacing income. One of the more curious findings is what happens to the annual replacement rate for households with annual incomes of less than $10,000 (15 percent of those unemployed): these households seem to have a bimodal distribution in their ability to replace income. Fifty-two percent of those with income less than $10,000 have replacement rates less than 0.8 but 19 percent have replacement rates greater than or equal to 1. A possible explanation of this distribution is that households with low total family income are more likely to have experienced longer durations of unemployment and consequently will have lower replacement rates. At the same time workers earning low wages have a smaller absolute income loss when unemployed and, therefore, are more likely even with limited social welfare payments to successfully "replace" lost income than workers with higher earning power. An alternative explanation of the distribution of these numbers is the way in which replacement rate is defined. It is assumed in table 5–1 (see table footnote b) that individuals would not receive food stamps or Aid to Families with Dependent Children (AFDC) if they experienced no unemployment during the survey year. However, assuming that households with annual income less than $10,000 a year would still receive AFDC and food stamps even when continuously employed, the percentage of households with annual replacement rates greater than or equal to 1 declines from 19 percent to 12 percent.

Determinants of the Probability of Having Experienced Unemployment

Since today more than 60 percent of all husband-wife households in the United States have more than one person in the labor force it is important when discussing married male unemployment to take into account the effect of a wife's labor market experience. In order to better understand the economic hardship of unemployment, this section focuses on the married respondents in the 1981 NLS Young Men's Cohort in order to determine the factors which influence the respondent's probability of being unemployed (conditional on being economically active) sometime during the survey year. A range of variables may influence this probability. Human capital variables such as the level of educational attainment and training might be expected to lessen the probability of a person's having been unemployed because of the higher demand for the trained person's services. Additional factors such as race, health, proxies for experience (age and age squared), and residence in a Standard Metropolitan Statistical Area (SMSA) or not, may also affect the demand for an individual's labor. The number of children in the household and the spouse's level of education are included as additional proxies for socioeconomic status. It is anticipated that those households with more than

Table 5–1
Percentage Distributions of Annual Household Replacement Rates by Race, Household Type, Duration of Unemployment, and Annual Family Income

| | | Characteristics | | | | | |
| | | Race | | Household Type | | | |
Percentage of Sample with Replacement Rate	Total	White	Black	1	2	3	4
<0.5	7.7	7.2	11.5	5.1	13.9	10.6	0.0
≥0.5 and <0.6	1.6	1.4	4.2	2.2	1.6	0.0	0.0
≥0.6 and <0.7	4.6	4.2	8.1	4.0	4.2	8.0	0.0
≥0.7 and <0.8	10.8	11.2	8.2	8.5	15.3	13.5	11.5
≥0.8 and <0.9	21.7	20.9	26.9	23.6	17.1	24.7	0.0
≥0.9 and <1.0	47.2	48.4	36.2	50.8	42.3	32.4	86.7
≥1.0	6.4	6.7	4.7	5.8	5.6	10.8	1.8
Mean household replacement rate	.88	.88	.83	.90	.83	.84	.94
Standard deviation	.16	.16	.20	.13	.21	.19	.08
Percentage of sample	100.0	88.6	10.6	60.6	20.2	16.2	3.0

Household type 1 = Married household, respondent and spouse in labor force.
Household type 2 = Unmarried respondent, respondent in labor force.
Household type 3 = Married household, only respondent in labor force.
Household type 4 = Married household, only spouse in labor force.

one worker may have both higher incidence and duration of unemployment because of an increase in the amount of wage income from other sources. A dummy variable is therefore included which indicates whether or not both the respondent and his spouse are economically active. Also included in the equation is unearned income, but the impact of unearned income (rental income, interest, dividends, alimony, child support, and so on) on the labor market behavior of male respondents is somewhat ambiguous. On the one hand, greater unearned income can subsidize longer job search. On the other hand, members of those households with greater amounts of unearned income are more likely to have been continuously employed, in which case unearned income may simply proxy for previous labor market experience.

Because the model being analyzed has a discrete dependent variable, efficiency can be improved by using logit maximum likelihood estimation. Table 5–2 presents, for married male respondents, findings on the determinants of the probability of experiencing any unemployment during the survey year.

In table 5–2 factors which decrease significantly the probability of a married respondent experiencing unemployment include his educational attainment, his training, and his spouse's education. These findings suggest that the accumulation of human capital plays an important role in the labor market

	Characteristics								
	Duration of Unemployment (Weeks)					Annual Family Income			
0–4	4–14	12–24	24–36	36+	$10,000	$10–20,000	$20–30,000	$30–40,000	$40,000+
3.8	1.4	2.8	12.1	34.0	23.6	5.7	4.7	0.0	9.9
0.0	0.0	1.2	3.3	8.2	7.4	0.8	1.0	0.0	0.0
0.0	0.0	3.5	11.8	20.0	7.4	3.6	3.8	8.1	0.0
0.0	7.3	21.3	24.1	11.8	13.2	17.3	7.4	6.6	0.0
1.3	33.1	40.7	20.1	16.7	11.7	22.4	26.0	25.9	16.0
85.0	50.4	27.9	19.5	9.3	18.0	47.2	54.7	50.7	67.4
9.9	7.8	2.6	9.1	0.0	18.7	3.0	2.4	8.7	6.7
.98	.92	.84	.77	.66	.78	.88	.90	.91	.95
.03	.10	.11	.21	.20	.28	.15	.10	.11	.05
30.3	23.1	22.8	11.7	12.1	15.1	33.5	26.5	15.7	9.2

experience of individuals. The significance of the spouse's educational level in the respondents' equation may simply be an additional proxy for socioeconomic status. At the same time the spouse's labor force participation does not appear to make it any more likely for the respondent to experience unemployment.

The impact of each independent variable on the probability of unemployment cannot be seen from the coefficients in table 5–2. To obtain a better idea of the impact of selected variables, I calculate in table 5–3 the probabilities for different types of individuals. Table 5–3 highlights the importance of human capital variables for the labor market experience of the married male respondents. In addition table 5–3 shows the dramatic rise in the probability of unemployment for those with "disadvantaged" characteristics.

Determinants of the Proportion of Time Unemployed

While the previous analysis gives some indication of the characteristics of the unemployed, it does not distinguish between the unemployment experience of long-term and short-term unemployed. To examine this issue more

Table 5–2
Logit Maximum Likelihood Estimates for the Determinants of
Unemployment Probabilities for Married Respondents

	Coefficient	Standard Error	Asymptotic t-Test
Independent variables			
Race	0.22	0.17	1.29
Highest grade completed	−0.07	0.019	−3.68
Training	−0.45	0.18	−2.50
Health	0.28	0.23	1.22
Number of children	0.04	0.06	0.67
Spouse's highest grade completed	−0.06	0.015	−4.00
Unearned income (in 100s)	−0.003	0.005	−0.6
Multiple-worker household	−0.027	0.15	−0.18
Age	−0.13	0.30	−0.43
Age-squared	0.002	0.008	0.25
SMSA	−0.145	0.148	−0.98
Constant	1.24	2.73	0.45

Note: number of cases = 1,910 (analysis on unweighted sample).

Table 5–3
Unemployment Probabilities for Respondent by Selected Characteristics

	Probability (%)
Typical[a]	7.0
Typical but:	
Highest grade completed = 10	8.0
No training	10.0
Highest grade completed by spouse = 10	7.4
Disadvantaged	22.5

[a]Where a "typical" married male respondent is white; has 13 years of schooling, training, good health, and 1.8 children; spouse has 12 years of schooling; unearned income = $457; spouse works; respondent was 18 in 1967 and lives in an SMSA. "Disadvantaged" respondents are black; have 10 years of schooling, no training, poor health, and 4 children; spouse has 10 years of schooling; no unearned income; spouse is not economically active; respondent was 18 in 1967 and lives in an SMSA.

closely, this section presents findings on the determinants of the proportion of time spent unemployed by the married respondent during the survey year conditional on having experienced unemployment during that time period. Because of data constraints with the NLS Young Men's Cohort, only the proportion of time spent unemployed in the survey year could be calculated, not unemployment by spell. However, the proportion of time spent unemployed may be a more appropriate variable to examine if the subject is the economic hardship experienced by the unemployed. According to Akerlof and Main (1980), in the United States many persons experience repeated spells of unemployment. Examining only the duration of unemployment of these repeatedly unemployed persons and ignoring its incidence may lead to understatement of the extent of such persons' unemployment experience.

In examining the proportion of time spent unemployed, job search theory can be used to identify variables which may influence the number of weeks spent unemployed over the survey year. In a simple job search model the probability that a worker will become reemployed can be viewed as the product of two probabilities: the probability of receiving a job offer and the probability of accepting a job offer. The probability of accepting a job offer will depend on the reservation wage. The reservation wage, w^*, is the wage which equates the expected discounted lifetime utility of accepting a job at wage w^* to the expected discounted lifetime utility of continuing at least one more period without employment. The reservation wage, in turn, depends upon the known wage offer distribution, the costs of search, any unemployment income, other sources of income (including spouse's earnings), and the probability of receiving a job offer. Given the distribution of wage offers, the factors most likely to influence the probability of receiving a job offer are local demand conditions (proxied here by the local SMSA unemployment rate in 1981) and personal characteristics, including ethnicity and human capital variables such as education and training, and health of the respondent.

A variable which is assumed to have a direct effect on the reservation wage but not on the probability of receiving a job offer is the young man's replacement ratio, that is, his ratio of average weekly unemployment income to his expected weekly earnings. To calculate the denominator of this ratio, we use an estimated earnings equation and calculate expected gross weekly earnings for each unemployed respondent given his own characteristics.[3]

Also included as determinants of the duration of unemployment are unearned income, annual income from the spouse, and a dummy variable for whether or not the household consisted of multiple workers. All these factors should influence the reservation wage. As income from all other sources increases, the respondent's reservation wage will increase; therefore, the duration of unemployment will increase unless unearned income proxies for previous labor market experience. If so, unearned income could be negatively related to the proportion of time unemployed.

Various assumptions can be made about the relationship between the spouse's annual income and her husband's unemployment experience. These assumptions determine the direction of the bias (or lack of bias) on the spouse's annual income coefficient. For instance, Heckman and Macurdy (1980) find little evidence of changes in married female labor supply responses to "transitory" shocks in household income due to the unemployment of their spouse. This would suggest that simultaneity bias is not a serious problem in the present model. However, if there is an added worker effect, as Lundberg (1985) has found, then the coefficient on spouse's annual income may be biased upward. This is conditional on the fact that not only does the wife decide to participate in the labor market due to her husband's unemployment but also that she is able to find employment. Evidence such as that presented by Heckman (1981) suggests that as the overall economy worsens, married women's employment *decreases*.

Testing for the sensitivity of the results is done by including the log of unemployment income and the log of expected earnings separately as well as in difference form. Table 5–4 reports the results of both specifications in equations (1) and (2). The two variables which appear to be significant determinants of a married young man's proportion of time unemployed are *Log Unemployment Income* and *Spouse's Annual Income*. These results seem to suggest that the unemployment experience of these young men is cushioned not only by unemployment income, but also by the contribution a wife makes to total household income.[4] In equation (2) the elasticity of the proportion of time unemployed with respect to *Unemployment Income* is 0.14, and the elasticity of the proportion of time spent unemployed with respect to *Spouse's Annual Income* is 0.08. To better understand what these elasticities imply

Table 5–4
OLS Estimates of the Determinants of Respondent's Proportion of Time Unemployed in Survey Year

	Equation 1		Equation 2	
	Coefficient	t-Test	Coefficient	t-Test
Independent variables				
Race	0.08	0.44	0.16	0.90
Education	−0.01	−0.55	−0.03	−1.08
Training	0.24	1.22	0.20	0.99
Health	0.30	1.22	0.25	1.01
Local unemployment rate	0.002	0.82	0.002	0.87
Spouse's annual income	0.0003	1.81	0.000029	1.68
Multiple worker household	−0.32	−1.60	−0.31	−1.55
Unearned income	−0.00002	−0.22	−0.00001	−0.10
Log replacement ratio	0.13	4.62	—	—
Log unemployment income	—	—	0.14	4.79
Log expected wage	—	—	0.43	1.64
Constant	−1.571	−4.10	−4.06	−3.36
R^2		0.16		0.18

Note: Number of cases = 188.
Dependent variable = log (proportion of survey year unemployed).

about the number of weeks the respondent remains unemployed, we can construct the following scenarios. Suppose the mean weekly unemployment income is $150 and it is increased by $50 per week (a 33 percent increase). The proportion of time spent unemployed at the mean would rise 4.7 percent from 17 percent of the survey year to 18 percent of the survey year. Although the number of weeks between interviews varies, for most respondents the survey year is approximately 52 weeks. This means that for the average unemployed respondent, the proportion of time spent unemployed would increase from 8.8 weeks to 9.4 weeks if he was given a $50 a week increase in unemployment income. This does not seem to be a particularly large increase given the size of the increase in unemployment income.

A 33 percent increase in the spouse's annual income (approximately $30 per week for 52 weeks) would increase the proportion of time spent unemployed by her husband by 2.6 percent. This implies at the mean a rise from 17 percent to 17.5 percent or 8.8 weeks to 9.1 weeks. Again, this is not a very large increase. So while both of these variables are significant, their overall impact on the proportion of time unemployed is relatively small.

The results presented in table 5-4 can be compared to other similar studies. Johnson (1983) attempted to develop a household model of unemployment and found using data from the 1975 *Current Population Survey* that a wife's income was a significant determinant of her husbands' duration of unemployment. However, she found that unemployment income was an insignificant determinant. Ehrenberg and Oaxaca (1976), using the four cohorts from the NLS, found that for the Young Men's Cohort in 1966–69, unemployment income did have a significant impact on the duration of unemployment. However, because of the ages of the cohort in those years, Ehrenberg and Oaxaca did not study the impact of spouse's income on the duration of unemployment of these young men. They also found, as I did, that while unemployment income was a significant determinant of the duration of unemployment, the size of its effect was quite small.

Conclusions

The previous sections indicate that households with only a single worker have greater difficulty than multiple worker households in replacing income over the survey year. While a spouse's labor force participation did not make it any more likely that her husband would experience unemployment, the amount of her annual income was a significant determinant of the proportion of time her husband spent unemployed. Another result found is that human capital variables play an important role in the probability that an individual will experience unemployment, and once unemployed, that unemployment income affects the duration of unemployment of married men aged 29–39.

Although both unemployment income and annual income from the spouse increase the amount of time spent unemployed, the elasticities imply that large increases in either source of income do not change the average number of weeks spent unemployed by a great amount. In conclusion, these results seem to indicate that policymakers who are interested in examining the relationship between unemployment and economic hardship should not ignore the impact of the presence of other household workers on the unemployment experience of married men.

Notes

1. In other words, I do not differentiate those women who have been in the labor force continuously during the survey from those who perhaps have been in the labor force for only 1 month out of the survey year.

2. Numerator = respondent's annual income from (wage + salary + business income + unemployment compensation + supplementary benefits + veteran's compensation + worker's compensation + social security disability payments + other disability payments) + farm income + rent + interest + food stamps + AFDC + Supplemental Social Security Income + child support and alimony + other income + income from other household members).

Denominator = same as numerator, but omitting income from unemployment compensation, supplementary benefits, food stamps, AFDC, Supplementary Social Security Income and replacing this sum with the number of weeks unemployed * average weekly hours * hourly wage rate (from current or last job).

Note that these income figures are not net-of-tax because we are not able to identify the state the respondent is from. The NLS contain data on whether changes in geographic location occurred over time, but the locations themselves are never coded.

3. The dependent variable in the earnings equation is the log of the wage in current or last job. Most of those unemployed during the survey year were employed at the survey date; but for those who were unemployed at the survey date, 60 percent reported a wage earned within the last 3 months. By defining the dependent variable in the earnings equation as the wage rate in the most recent employment and by using a fitted value from the earnings equation to construct the denominator of the replacement ratio, I hoped to avoid problems of endogeneity. If fitted values from an earnings equation based on only those employed were used to construct the denominator or if an individual's actual income either pre- or postunemployment were used, endogeneity could be a problem.

4. Interpretation of these results is complicated, however, since we have not explicitly taken into account the problem of unobserved heterogeneity (see Heckman and Borjas, 1980, and Flinn and Heckman, 1982), that is, the bias introduced by the omission of unobservable variables such as motivation.

References

Akerlof, G.A., and B.G.M. Main. 1980. "Unemployment Spells and Unemployment Experience." *American Economic Review* (Dec.):885–893.

Ehrenberg, R., and R. Oaxaca. 1976. "Unemployment Insurance, Duration of Unemployment, and Subsequent Wage Gain." *American Economic Review:*754–766.

Flinn, C., and J. Heckman. 1982. "Models for the Analysis of Labor Force Dynamics." In *Advances in Econometrics.* Greenwich, Conn.: JAI Press, pp. 35–95.

Heckman, J. 1981. "Heterogeneity and State Dependence." In S. Rosen, ed., *Studies in Labor Markets,* Chicago: University of Chicago Press, pp. 91–140.

———— and G. Borjas. 1980. "Does Unemployment Cause Further Unemployment? Definitions, Questions, and Answers from a Continuous Time Model of Heterogeneity and State Dependence." *Economica* (Aug.):247–283.

———— and T. Macurdy. 1980. "A Life Cycle Model of Female Labour Supply." *Review of Economic Studies:*47–74.

Johnson, J. 1983. "Unemployment as a Household Labor Supply Decision." *Quarterly Review of Economics and Business* (Summer):71–88.

Lippmann, S., and J. McCall. 1976. "The Economics of Job Search: A Survey." *Economic Inquiry:*155–189.

Lundberg, S. 1985. "The Added Worker Effect." *The Journal of Labor Economics.*

Mortenson, D.T. 1970. "Job Search, The Duration of Unemployment and Phillips Curve." *American Economic Review* (Dec.):847–862.

6
Career Mobility among Young Men: A Search for Patterns

Janina C. Latack
Ronald J. D'Amico

S tudies of career mobility have emphasized socioeconomic advancement and have researched the topic primarily from the human capital (Becker, 1975) and structuralist perspectives (Doeringer and Piore, 1971; Edwards, 1975). Recently there has been increased interest in the patterns of job changes which make up individual careers (Felmlee, 1982; Jacobs, 1983; Kalleberg and Hudis, 1979). Using a model which incorporates human capital, structural, and psychological variables, this chapter examines the determinants of career mobility among young men over a 15-year period.

Models of Career Mobility

Two issues arise in considering models of career mobility: How do we define it? And what are its determinants? A large body of research investigates human capital variables as determinants of career mobility (Becker, 1975). These models emphasize individual attributes, arguing that socioeconomic advancement depends upon increases in the store of human capital that workers offer to the labor market—work experience, on-the-job training, formal training programs, and additional education. The structuralist approach, on the other hand, deemphasizes individual attributes in favor of the opportunity structure within which the individual's job is embedded. Examples are dual labor market theory (Doeringer and Piore, 1971) and dual economy theory (Edwards, 1975). Both models emphasize demand-side factors, including a fundamental cleavage and limited mobility between a primary or core sector and a secondary or peripheral sector. The primary sector is characterized by long promotional ladders and opportunities for advancement, the secondary by short or nonexistent promotional ladders and limited opportunities for advancement or skill development.

Other recent viewpoints (Beck, Horan, and Tolbert, 1978; Bibb and Form, 1977; Spilerman, 1977) project more complex labor market structures but share with dualist models the view that careers are shaped fundamentally by the labor markets within which they develop. Because of the presumed high costs of career switching and the limited branching options associated with any job, the different features of these labor markets give rise to powerful career trajectories set in motion with early labor market experiences (see D'Amico and Golon, chapter 2 of this book). Empirical models drawing on the structuralist perspective assign particular importance to the role of occupation and the industry or firm attributes of one's current or initial employment (Grandjean, 1981; Rosenbaum, 1979).

Career adjustment necessarily derives from both individual and structural factors, however, so models of career mobility that emphasize either structural or individual factors may misrepresent the interactive nature of the process. To provide a more complete picture of career mobility, the model developed here incorporates both human capital and structural factors, along with motivational characteristics.

The majority of career mobility studies define the dependent variable—socioeconomic advancement—rather narrowly, as growth in wages or occupational status. However, this definition omits an interesting facet of career mobility—the type and frequency of job-related changes over the course of the career. Various combinations of employer and occupational change are also implied in the term *career mobility,* particularly in our present economic climate where individuals will need to make an increasing number of job-related changes in response to structural economic changes. Recent studies have begun to explore this dimension of career mobility by mapping intrafirm and interfirm job moves (Felmlee, 1982; Jacobs, 1983; Latack and Shaw, 1983; Kalleberg and Hudis, 1979).

Career progression has many dimensions, and we aim to capture several of these dimensions in the definition of the dependent variable. A recent typology of career patterns that incorporates type and frequency of job change (Driver, 1983) serves as a mechanism for creating our multidimensional variable of career mobility. Driver has defined four common career patterns, or "career concepts," which capture predominant themes observed as careers unfold over time in this society. The four concepts are: linear, steady state, transitory, and spiral. The *linear* career emphasizes early occupational choice followed by a series of predominantly upward moves. The key aspect is evidence of upward movement as reflected in additional job responsibility and income. The *steady-state* individual also makes an early choice, but the key ingredient is low frequency of change. Although there may be growth in income and skill, the essential factor is little movement over the course of the career. The *transitory* career pattern is characterized by frequent choices, so that no job or field is ever permanently chosen. Changes of employer or occupation occur as frequently as every 1 or 2 years and are mainly lateral. In the *spiral* career, the individual develops within a given field for some time and then makes a change, possibly a major change, in cycles of 5 to 10 years. There may be upward movement within a cycle, but the shift between cycles is often lateral. The spiral pattern is a particularly contemporary phenomenon brought about in part by the increasing incidence and acceptability of relatively major reorientations at various points in an individual's career.[1] Driver's typology also acknowledges that careers may combine more than one pattern over time.

Driver further notes that these career concepts are strongly rooted in relatively stable motivational characteristics and needs which give rise to preferences for amount and type of movement. For the linear individual, the key need is for achievement as reflected in wealth, power, and movement up the ladder. For the steady-state individual, the key motivating factors are security and respect. For the transitory, there are strong needs for independence and variety. For the spiral, achievement, defined in terms of self-actualization and growth, is the key motive. These motives, though they may be imperfectly realized due to labor market and organizational constraints, are viewed as influential in determining the career pattern that is established. The importance of motivational factors has, in fact, been highlighted in recent expansions of the human capital model, most notably by Andrisani (1977).

The model presented in figure 6–1 is offered as a more comprehensive picture of career mobility over time because it incorporates human capital, structural and motivational variables as determinants and it portrays career mobility in the composite manner suggested by the Driver (1983) typology. The present analysis also represents an advantage over other career mobility studies because data are examined over a 15-year period instead of at two or three points in time as in Jacobs (1983) or Kalleberg and Hudis (1979).

Hypotheses

Predictions about the determinants of career pattern can be derived from the various theoretical models described in the preceding section.

Education and Work Experience Variables

Human capital theory predicts that additional education and work experience will be important determinants of career pattern.

The Linear Career Pattern. In the human capital perspective, the effect of additional education should be positive in a linear career pattern. The effect of work experience should also be positive, because, according to human capital theory, workers invest heavily in on-the-job training early in a career (Lazear, 1976) and later reap returns from these efforts. The effect of aging,

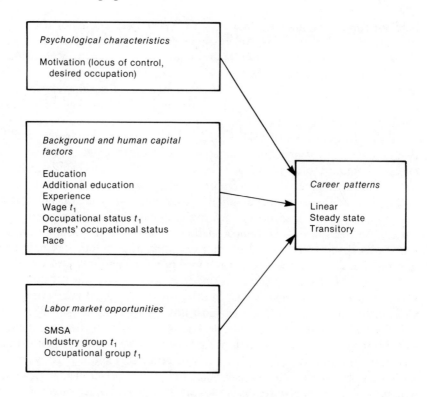

Figure 6–1. Determinants of Career Patterns

however, suggests that years in the work force will be negatively related to a linear career because additional human capital investments tend to taper off as workers approach midcareer. Thus, over time, evidence of a linear career should decline.

The Steady-State Career Pattern. Because acquisition of additional education usually leads to upward movement, one would not expect additional education to be a characteristic of a steady-state career pattern. The effect of work experience on a steady-state career may also be positive simply because it reflects stability of employment and commitment to a career. In addition, the aging effect necessarily suggests a positive connection between time in the work force and a steady-state pattern, a connection also suggested by empirical evidence that upward mobility declines as workers age (Jacobs, 1983).

The Transitory Career Pattern. In the transitory pattern, the lack of commitment to a particular course may be expressed in a lack of perserverence needed to complete additional education; thus the education variable should be negatively associated with a transitory pattern. The human capital investment proxied by work experience would suggest that, over time, workers use this experience to advantage either by reaping firm-internal rewards or by making advantageous moves, neither of which characterize the transitory pattern. Thus the relationship between work experience and the transitory pattern should be negative.

Motivation Variables

Concerning motivational determinants, both Driver (1983) and Andrisani (1977) have suggested that locus of control could be an important variable. *Locus of control* denotes the individual perceptions concerning control of rewards (Rotter, 1966). A person with an internal locus of control perceives success as contingent upon personal effort and initiative, whereas a person with an external locus of control views success as more independent of effort and more likely to result from external circumstances or luck. As Andrisani pointed out, locus of control is a particularly important individual attribute to consider in work history analysis because it reflects a value system ingrained by the Protestant work ethic. In addition, there is considerable empirical support for the *expectancy theory of motivation* (Vroom, 1964), which emphasizes the importance of perceived payoff to effort. Motivation may also be reflected in occupational aspirations the individual holds at a young age. Thus, an internal locus of control and high occupational aspirations should be predictive of a linear career. Since the transitory person is motivated by a need for independence and variety, then internal locus of control should also be a positive factor for this pattern. Because there is a lack of emphasis on occupational commitment, however, occupational aspirations may be unimportant or perhaps negatively related to the transitory pattern. The need for security and respect from others suggests that a more external locus of control should be predictive of a steady-state career. On the other hand, there may be many ambitious individuals who aim for steady-state careers in medicine or law or other professions which require considerable initiative, particularly in the early years when the individual is in school. Thus, a counterargument could be made that internal locus of control and high occupational aspirations might also characterize the steady-state pattern.

Labor Market Structural Variables

The structuralist theories attach importance to the initial choice which place the individual within an opportunity structure that establishes a career trajectory and determines subsequent career pattern. One implication of these theories, particularly in the dualist view, is that the die is cast—that is, there is little mobility between labor market sectors and the initial trajectory is so powerful that it leads to the development of poor work habits which further ensure that the person stays mired in the secondary sector. If this theory is correct, then the variables which serve as a proxy for labor market structure at the beginning of the career should be important predictors of subsequent career pattern; that is, the industry and occupation in which the person begins a career should have an influence. Industries in the peripheral sector should be positively associated with transitory careers and negatively associated with linear careers. The association of core-versus-periphery distinctions with the steady-state pattern is more ambiguous, however, because some steady-state careers accrue to individuals in the primary sector (physicians, lawyers, and other professionals), while other steady-state career patterns are found among clerks and bookkeepers in the low-wage, dead-end jobs that characterize the secondary sector. Although the core and periphery sectors have been classified by industry (Beck et al., 1978; Bibb and Form, 1977), there is little agreement about whether or not classifying by industry is the best method of operationalizing the concepts of core and periphery sector. Jacobs (1983) has argued that occupation has a more constraining effect on career mobility than does industry. These considerations suggest that both industry and occupation should be examined as determinants of career mobility patterns.

One final aspect of labor market structure concerns the population of the geographic area. Mobility opportunities should be more plentiful in more populated areas, which suggests that working in a metropolitan area, net of other factors, may preview a linear or transitory career because there would be more opportunities for mobility of all kinds; thus the effect for a steady state is expected to be negative, indicating that those working in less populated areas tend to establish less mobile careers. Since populated areas offer more opportunities for advancement, however, we would expect a positive effect for a linear career.

Methodology

The career patterns identified by Driver (1983) are operationalized by comparing the hourly wage (adjusted to 1981 dollars), occupation, and employer of the survey week for jobs held in consecutive pairs of interview years in which the respondent was employed but not enrolled in school. Respondents were interviewed 12 times between 1966 and 1981, so there are 11 possible pairwise comparisons.[2] Each comparison was classified according to whether or not it primarily suggested a linear, transitory, or steady-state career. Only respondents for whom at least 5 pairwise comparisons were possible were retained for this analysis. This restriction was applied to ensure that each respondent had a sufficient number of comparison years available for examining career development over time. To lessen confounding of results by period effects, only those respondents whose terminal year was 1981 were retained. This implies that the respondent had to be employed and interviewed in 1981 and have valid data for relevant job characteristics. When these restrictions were imposed, 1,666 respondents remained for analysis.

Classifying any given pairwise comparison as linear, transitory, or steady state was necessarily arbitrary. The following criteria were used.

1. If the respondent realized an above-average increase in hourly wage over the period t to $t + 1$ or if his $t + 1$ occupation showed a net increase of level of complexity in dealing with data, people, things, or intelligence, then the comparison was labeled linear.[3]

2. If the comparison did not meet criterion 1, but if the person did not realize a decline in actual wages or job responsibility over the period and stayed with the time t occupation or employer, then the comparison was labeled steady state.

3. If the comparison was not labeled linear and involved a simultaneous change of employer and occupation, then the job change was labeled transitory.

These three criteria constitute a mutually exclusive but not necessarily exhaustive coding of all pairwise comparisons. Summing codings of all pairwise comparisons for each respondent created three variables: percentage of comparisons coded linear, percentage coded steady state, and percentage coded transitory. While the coding of any given pairwise comparison involves somewhat arbitrary decision rules, it is believed that the aggregate scores for each individual capture fundamental differences in job mobility patterns across respondents along several dimensions.

Two other definitions of the linear pattern and one other definition of the transitory were also created. Since a key aspect of linearity is upward movement in wages and responsibility, the net change on wages and job responsibility from t_1 to 1981 were taken as additional operational definitions of linearity. The wage-growth variable represents an average annual percent change in wages and corresponds to measures of wage growth used elsewhere (Duncan, 1979).[4] The second additional measure of linearity is the difference in job responsibility scores (as measured by data, people, things, and intelligence (see note 3) from t to 1981), divided by the number of years elapsed.

A second operational definition of the transitory pattern was the percentage of years in which there was a change of employers. Given that the early career stage is characterized by exploration and trying out, we can further study the evidence of transitoriness by noting that although lack of wage growth may accompany a transitory career pattern, the most important dimension according to Driver's (1983) theory is *frequency* of movement, that is, the notion of never being "settled in". Hence, the person who changes employers more frequently has a more transitory career than the person for whom employer change is less common.

In addition to demographic and background variables, the standard human capital variables are included: education, additional education, and work experience, proxied by weeks unemployed. This proxy was chosen so that unemployment, a common variable of interest in studies of mobility, could be discussed. In our subsample, weeks worked is the approximate inverse of weeks unemployed, so the measure in effect shows the number of weeks an individual could not accumulate work experience. Aging effects were measured by the time elapsed from the point of entry into the sample (see note 2) and 1981. A series of variables reflective of motivation and labor market opportunities were also defined. Motivation was proxied by locus of control (Rotter, 1966),[5] and occupational aspirations as indicated by status of occupation aspired to at age 30 as reported in 1966, using Duncan's (1961) index.

Labor market structure was represented by several variables. A series of dummy variables based on industry and occupation at t_1 were created, using one-digit classifications of the U.S. Bureau of the Census (1960). In addition, whether the individual was in a Standard Metropolitan Statistical Area (SMSA) in the first year as well as the percentage of years spent in an SMSA were taken to reflect that workers in more populated areas may have more opportunity for mobility.

Results

Sample Description

A description of the sample as a whole and by race is provided in table 6–1. The average age of the respondents is 21 in the first year and 34 in 1981. Only 1 percent of the sample was over age 27 at the starting year. The average respondent is a high school graduate who started out earning approximately $7.00 (in 1981 dollars) per hour. After a 3.4 percent average annual growth in hourly wage, the 1981 wage is $10.67. Just over 24 percent of the unweighted sample is black. While occupational status increased during the 15-year period, the status of the current occupation on average falls well below that of the desired occupation reported in 1966. Employer changes were made in 35 percent of the years.[6]

For the sample as a whole, by far the most predominant career pattern is

Table 6–1
Sample Description: Total and by Race

Independent Variables	Total (N = 1,666)		Black (N = 408)		White (N = 1,258)	
	$\overline{X}$	s.d.	$\overline{X}$	s.d.	$\overline{X}$	s.d.
Age-t_1	21.1	2.6	20.8	2.6	21.1	2.6
Age-1981	34.3	3.0	34.3	3.2	34.3	3.0
Education-t_1	12.6	2.6	11.5	2.6	12.8	2.5
Education-1981	13.2	2.5	12.1	2.6	13.3	2.5
Wage-t_1[a]	6.94	2.93	5.36	2.54	7.14	2.91
Wage-1981[a]	10.67	4.55	7.94	3.74	11.01	4.50
Hourly wage growth[b]	3.4	3.7	3.0	4.0	3.4	3.6
Occupational status-t_1	36.3	24.6	24.6	21.3	37.7	24.6
Occupational status-1981	44.6	24.8	29.5	22.4	46.5	24.5
Desired occupational status	53.4	24.7	44.5	27.1	54.5	24.3
Locus of control	22.4	5.4	24.6	5.6	22.1	5.3
Employer changes[c]	34.5	21.3	35.6	21.0	34.3	21.3
Weeks unemployed	2.4	4.7	4.1	6.4	2.2	4.4
Career pattern[d]						
Linear	70.9	15.2	69.7	15.3	71.0	15.2
Steady state	14.8	13.5	14.8	13.1	14.7	13.6
Transitory	4.1	7.8	4.2	7.7	4.1	7.8

[a]In 1981 dollars per hour.
[b]Annual average percentage growth in hourly wage t_1-1981.
[c]Percentage of years respondent changed employers.
[d]Percentage of years respondent showed evidence of the career pattern.

linear, with the average young man showing evidence of linearity in 70 percent of the comparison years. The corresponding mean for steady state is nearly 15 percent of the years, and for transitory the percentage is only 4.1 percent.

The breakdown by race shows that although the two subgroups are relatively close in age at both points in time, blacks start out behind whites in both hourly wage and occupational status and fall farther behind over time. The average annual hourly wage growth per year is 3 percent for blacks and 3.4 percent for whites. Blacks start out earning approximately $2.00 per hour less than whites, and by 1981 the gap is over $3.00 per hour. Blacks have spent nearly twice as many weeks unemployed. Race differences in frequencies of the three career patterns are not striking.

The sample distribution across the three career patterns, shown graphically in figure 6–2, indicates that for the majority of the sample, linearity is

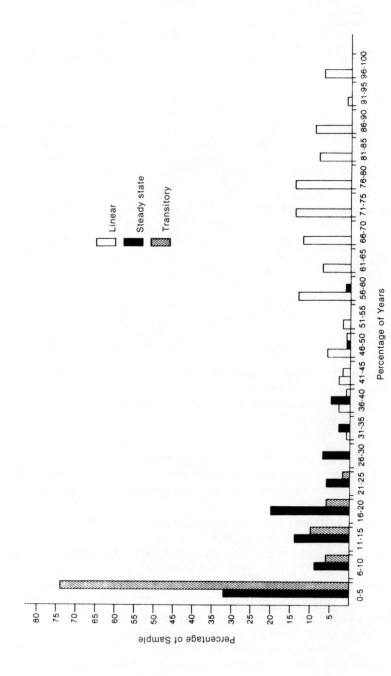

Figure 6–2. Sample Distribution across Career Patterns

shown in over half of the years. In contrast, a steady-state or transitory pattern is shown far less frequently, with nearly three-fourths of the sample showing no transitory years at all and approximately one-third of the sample showing no steady-state years.

This profile of career patterns shows that young men's careers are characterized by strong upward mobility as indicated by above-average wage gain and increased responsibility. They are not, however, making many transitory shifts as they have been defined here (employer-occupation shifts accompanied by below average wage gains). Thus, despite the fact that these men are in the early stages of their careers, occupation and employer switching suggestive of exploratory searching for the right job (Super, 1957) is not common. Given that, on average, these young men changed employers over one-third of the time, it appears that this type of shift was frequently accompanied by above-average wage gains rather than floundering or trying out different entry level jobs. The relative infrequency of steady-state years confirms the expectation that few of these young men stay in the same occupation with the same employer without strong gains in wages and responsibility.

The distribution of career patterns shows that 88.9 percent of the pairwise comparisons could be classified into one of the three patterns. The 11.1 percent of comparison years that could not be coded were those that did not meet the decision rules applicable to any of the three patterns. Cases excluded would be comparisons that showed a decline in wages without meeting the decision criteria to be coded transitory—for example, someone who left a previous employer, possibly involuntarily, someone whose subsequent job in the same occupation paid less compared with the previous job, or someone who experienced a cut in pay while staying in the same job.

Next we classify respondents into one of the three categories on the basis of predominant career patterns. In table 6–2 the sample is divided into those who most clearly approximate a modal type insofar as they show, relative to others in the sample, stronger evidence of a predominant pattern. This division was accomplished by considering the mean scores on the linear career pattern as a departure point because the sample as a whole shows a strongly linear pattern. Thus, one way of approximating a predominant pattern in Driver's model is to select that group of individuals who are above the sample mean of 70.9 percent on linear, select a second group who are above the mean of 14.7 percent on steady state but less than 70.9 on linear, and a third group who fall above the mean of 4.1 percent on transitory and who are not in the first two groups.

Looking at mean scores in table 6–2 we can see that while the age range is comparable across the three groups, educational differences are apparent. Those who ultimately establish a stronger transitory pattern start out and end up with less education than the other two groups, while educational differences among the linear and steady-state patterns appear inconsequential.

102 • *The Changing Labor Market*

Table 6–2
Sample Description by Predominant Career Pattern

Independent Variables	Linear (N = 877)		Steady State (N = 522)		Transitory (N = 133)	
	$\overline{X}$	s.d.	$\overline{X}$	s.d.	$\overline{X}$	s.d.
Age-t_1	21.0	2.6	21.4	2.6	20.6	2.7
Age-1981	34.0	3.0	34.7	3.0	34.0	3.1
Education-t_1	12.8	2.4	12.6	2.6	11.8	2.7
Education-1981	13.4	2.4	13.1	2.5	12.3	2.6
Wage-t_1[a]	6.79	2.82	7.06	2.91	6.80	3.10
Wage-1981[a]	11.26	4.56	10.31	2.72	8.80	4.28
Hourly wage growth[b]	4.1	3.7	2.8	3.4	1.8	3.7
Occupational status-t_1	36.0	22.6	37.8	24.6	31.0	22.2
Occupational status-1981	47.1	24.1	42.4	25.0	39.1	26.0
Desired occupational status	55.0	23.8	52.6	25.5	48.7	26.9
Locus of control	22.3	5.5	22.4	5.4	22.5	4.8
Employer changes[c]	35.2	21.2	28.8	18.3	53.6	21.4
Weeks unemployed	2.2	4.5	2.0	4.4	5.2	6.5
Career pattern[d]						
Linear	82.4	8.7	56.8	10.2	60.7	7.3
Steady state	8.6	9.0	29.4	10.8	5.9	5.9
Transitory	2.9	6.3	3.6	6.5	18.5	9.6

[a]In 1981 dollars per hour.
[b]Annual average percentage growth in hourly wage t_1-1981.
[c]Percentage of years respondent changed employers.
[d]Percentage of years respondent showed evidence of the career pattern.

Although the observed differences in wage growth reflect the manner in which the variables were empirically defined, it is interesting to note some initial differences in occupational status. Those who end up with transitory careers are in lower status occupations to begin with than either linear or steady-state individuals, but steady-state and linear individuals often start out in occupations of similar status.

While *locus of control* does not appear to differentiate the three groups, their aspirations, as reflected by status of desired occupation, show small differences, with those in linear career patterns having the highest aspirations, those in steady-state patterns intermediate, and those in transitory patterns the lowest. The trend of the data across the three groups lends some credence to the notion of career trajectories established early: the transitory pattern, characterized by low wage growth and instability, is previewed by a lower educational level to start, lower occupational aspirations, and lower initial occupational status.

Estimation Equations

The results for the estimation equations are presented in table 6–3. The patterns of coefficients which predict the three measures of upward mobility—linear; wage growth; Data, People, Things, and Intelligence (DPTI)—are somewhat similar.

The Linear Pattern. For a linear career pattern, the coefficient for starting wage is negative, starting education and additional education are positive, and years elapsed has a negative effect. The effect of occupational group and industry is not striking, though relative to the omitted categories the entertainment industry is less likely to foster linear careers while clerical and sales work is somewhat more likely to offer potential for a linear career.

Wage Growth. For wage growth the model is more clearly predictive, with some interesting differences compared with the linear pattern. Although the initial level of education is important, factors like initial occupational status, the initial advantage of having high status parents, moving to or working in an SMSA, and avoidance of excessive employer switching also make a positive contribution. The significant race coefficient indicates that wage-growth profiles for blacks are flatter, confirming that blacks fall farther behind in wages over time. The effect of industry and occupation is more noticeable: those who start out in agriculture, construction, finance, insurance, and real estate show stronger wage-growth trajectories than do public administration workers. Paradoxically, the professional and managerial groups as well as clerical and sales groups offer lower wage growth than the omitted category of unskilled blue-collar work. It may be that some of these young men ultimately reap dramatic wage gains through occupational switching at some later point.

DPTI. The Data, People, Things, and Intelligence coefficient indicates upward mobility reflected in increased responsibility and job complexity. Workers who entered the sample at an older age and those who have chosen higher status occupations are less likely to show upward mobility. This result may reflect the unwillingness of those who are older or in higher status occupations to switch occupations, a necessary action to score a change in DPTI. The positive effects of initial advantage are reflected in the positive coefficients for starting education and parental occupational status. The negative effect of unemployment is clear in that the more the worker has experienced unemployment, the lower the likelihood of moving up to jobs with higher responsibility. The industry effects emerge most strongly for DPTI, showing that choosing work in transportation, communication, utilities, mining, construction, and manufacturing pays off more than choosing work in the public sector in terms of growth in responsibility. These coefficients do support dual labor market theory insofar as they show that indus-

Table 6-3
Standardized Regression Coefficients for Career Patterns
(N = 1,274)

Independent Variables	Measures of Linear Career			Measure of Steady State Career	Measures of Transitory Career	
	(1) % Linear[a]	(2) Wage Growth	(3) DPTI Score	(4) % Steady State[a]	(5) % Transitory[a]	(6) Employer Changes
Age-t_1	-.04	-.05	-.06*	.03	-.04	-.05
Occupational status t_1	-.09	.25***	-.52***	.16*	-.03	-.09
Wage-t_1	-.17***	-.60***	.02	.04	.00	-.08*
Education t_1	.22***	.24***	.20***	-.05	-.10*	-.12**
Additional education	.10***	.02	.10***	-.07*	-.02	.04
Race (1 = white)	.04	.07***	.08***	-.03	.03	.04
SMSA-t_1	.04	-.11**	-.08+	-.08	.04	.07
Percentage of years in SMSA	.04	.20***	.06	.02	-.10+	-.08+
Parent's occupational status	-.03	.05+	.00	-.01	.04	.07**
Desired occupational status	.00	.04	.05+	.01	.00	.03
Locus of control	-.01	-.02	.00	-.03	.02	.05+
Different employers	—	-.07**	—	—	—	—
Weeks unemployed	-.03	-.03	-.09***	-.09***	.23***	.30***
Years elapsed	-.13*	-.01	-.06	.02	-.02	-.15**
Year entered industry[b]	.00	.07	-.03	-.10+	-.02	.00
Professional services	-.11	-.02	.02	-.01	-.01	.08*
Agriculture	-.02	.10***	.00	.00	.00	.09*

Transportation, communication and utilities	.05	.05	.09*	−.07+	−.00	.00
Mining	.03	.02	.04+	−.05	−.02	.03
Construction	.01	.07+	.07*	.00	.05	.18***
Manufacturing	.05	.00	.11*	−.05	.04	.07
Wholesale/retail trade	−.06	.06	.05	−.03	.05	.16***
Finance, insurance, real estate	−.02	.05+	.04	−.01	.04	.07*
Business and repair services	.02	.04	.02	.00	.04	.08**
Personal services	.00	.03	−.04	.03	.01	.08**
Entertainment	−.05+	.01	.00	.03	.06*	.05*
Occupational group[c]					.07*	.03
Professional and managerial	−.01	−.17**	−.13*	−.10	.09	.07
Clerical and sales	.07+	−.07*	.06	−.11+	−.00	.00
Skilled blue collar	.03	−.03	−.23***	.08	−.03	−.02
Constant	74.42	1.03	.21	19.68	8.30	64.42
R^2	.08	.34	.34	.05	.10	.22

[a] Percentage of years respondent showed evidence of this career pattern.
[b] Omitted category = public administration.
[c] Omitted category = unskilled and semiskilled blue collar.

+ Significant at .10.
* Significant at .05.
** Significant at .01.
*** Significant at .001.

tries differ in the degree of upward occupational mobility they offer. Recall that in order to score upward movement on the DPTI measure, one has to change occupations. Thus these coefficients reflect that making an initial choice of particular industries can affect later occupational change in an upward direction.

The importance of human capital investment for upward mobility is confirmed by these equations, not only human capital acquired after entering the labor force but also the initial store of human capital the young man possesses at the beginning of his career. Previous studies of wage growth have also found this strong effect for starting educational level (Duncan, 1979). Proponents of the human capital model such as Mincer (1970) have suggested that those who are well-educated to start may have developed the capacity to take advantage of work experience to move up. In addition, the results confirm the importance of additional education for achieving consistently strong wage growth and movement into more responsible jobs. Finally, while wage growth and movement into more responsibility does not taper off with years of experience, the strong upward movement characterized in the linear career pattern does level off relatively early. Recall that the mean age of the sample in 1981 was only 34. It may be that the leveling off in investment in on-the-job training predicted by human capital theory occurs at quite an early stage in men's careers.

The notion of a trajectory established by origin variables received some support more on the basis of initial occupational choice than on industry of origin. Initial occupational status previews wage growth and stability of occupational choice over time. In some cases, the industry coefficients, rather than connoting immobility, suggest upward mobility associated with certain industries (construction, mining, and manufacturing) and, as indicated in the DPTI equation, suggest occupational changes and perhaps movement out of those industries, probably in response to the economic fluctuations over this period.

Across the three equations examining upwardly mobile career patterns, the salience of motivational influences for upward mobility does not emerge. Thus, although motivational factors may be important in initial work-related choices over a shorter period of time (Andrisani, 1977), these effects do not appear as important over a longer time, particularly when they are compared with educational qualifications and labor market opportunity.

The Steady-State Pattern. The coefficients for the steady-state pattern show that entering a high status occupation does predict that pattern, while additional education is a negative predictor. It may be that both the quest for security and the early ambition that leads workers to enter high status occupations is at work. In other words, those who search for security would be less likely to seek further education, and additional formal education is less likely to be demanded of those, like lawyers, who enter high-status occupations initially. As would be expected, unemployment has a negative effect, even after controlling for other factors. Industry and occupational effects are virtually nonexistent.

The Transitory Pattern. Finally, a transitory career is more likely among those who start with less education and in nonurban areas. Unemployment is strongly associated with this pattern, indicating that bouts of unemployment are associated with changes of occupation and employer and below-average changes in wages. The industry effects are not strong here, but those that are observed are consistent with dual labor market theory insofar as industries with a substantial proportion of secondary market jobs (business and repair services and personal services) give rise to more transitory careers. Finally, the equation that models a transitory career pattern as reflected by frequency of employer change suggests that the transitory pattern which is accompanied by low wage growth is determined by different factors than employer changes alone. Starting wage and education have a negative effect, suggesting that those who start out in disadvantaged positions do indeed tend to move more often. This pattern is more characteristic of those in nonurban areas. Surprisingly, parental occupational status makes a positive contribution, as does an external locus of control. The positive effect for parental status is somewhat inconsistent with the disadvantaged position implied in the other coefficients as well as other studies (such as Treas and Tyree, 1979) which have found status transmission to be positive from parent to offspring. Perhaps this finding reflects the experience of that subset of young men who choose not to reap the expected payoffs from their high status origins.

Conclusions

The pattern of results suggests that being black is still a substantial liability. Unlike other studies which have argued that the wage differential between blacks and whites is narrowing (Lazear, 1976) or at least not increasing (Duncan, 1979), this study shows that blacks start out behind whites and show a slower rate of wage growth over time, even when human capital and labor market factors are controlled. This finding is noteworthy because the data span a longer period than previous studies and cover a cohort of young men who entered the labor force for the most part in the late 1960s, when one might expect to see a payoff to the implementation of civil rights legislation and affirmative action plans. Although the initial industry is not a major point of origin of one's career trajectory, the status of one's initial occupation choice does affect the career trajectory. The results support Jacob's (1983) argument that industry may be less controlling than occupation. In addition, while initial occupation may preview a career mobility pattern, the die may be cast even sooner, following a path carved by initial educational and parental advantage along with racial background. Thus, there are somewhat pessimistic aspects of these results, namely that the die seems to be cast even earlier than the structuralist theories would predict.

On a more optimistic note, however, working in a populated area was consistently related to career mobility patterns. Those moving to an SMSA or spending more of their career within an SMSA had more opportunity for wage growth and employer changes and less likelihood of establishing a transitory, low-wage-growth career. Given the fundamental structural changes occurring in many industrial sectors, it may be that workers were able to adapt, through retraining and movement to expanding industries, without the negative impacts of structural unemployment that have been predicted. When this adaptability is coupled with the positive effect of education, the picture that emerges is that factors within the control of the individual are perhaps more powerful than the influence of labor market structure that takes over after entry into a particular industry. In short, subsequent individual actions pay off regardless of the sector within which one begins a career.

Concerning individual initiative and motivation, assuming it to be a stable individual characteristic, the effects were not strong. It may be that, over time, individual initiative becomes reflected in other career-related choices (Mincer, 1970) such as the pursuit of additional education or moving to a more urban area to increase chances for mobility.

Finally, we have shown that expanding the conceptual definition of career mobility pattern to include type and frequency of job change along with the more standard view of socioeconomic attainment defined by wage growth is theoretically intriguing but correspondingly more difficult to predict. The variance explained by the model developed here was substantially higher for wage growth and employer change than for the more complex definitions of career pattern. One limitation of this study is that operationalizing the Driver (1983) typology was necessarily a compromise. For example, although the Rotter (1966) scale is one measure of motivation, it does not conform precisely to the scheme of needs that Driver has argued gives rise to patterns of mobility preferences. Similarly, individuals may move from job to job due to both motivational preferences and demand-side considerations, but the NLS data do not report their motives for job changes in all the comparison years. Job moves that offered growth in responsibility not accompanied by occupational change could not be adequately studied. Finally, the sample as a whole was so predominantly linear that there was little variance to be explained in the dependent variables. Although this finding is consistent with expectations about early career, it also limits the potential explanation of factors which contribute to career mobility patterns. It may be that the career patterns become more clearly visible only after people reach the midcareer period, suggesting that data over a longer time may be required to adequately observe these patterns.

In general, isolating the individual and structural factors giving rise to career patterns was difficult. It may be that for career patterns to be explained from objective work history data, we need still a longer time frame. In addition, people vary in their views of what it means to have a career or career pattern. We may need to combine people's subjective interpretations of their careers with analysis of objective work history data to complete the picture.

The identification of common career patterns indicated that young men were predominantly linear, showing a strong upwardly mobile pattern during the early to midcareer years. Steady-state and transitory career patterns were far less common. It did not seem to be the case that characteristics of the job held at the beginning of the period considered (that is, occupation or industry designation) gave rise to identifiable job sequences or were strongly associated with different rates of wage growth. In this sense, the rigid trajectories postulated by structuralist models did not prevail here.

These data argue for the timeworn admonitions to young people to stay in school and be willing to move to where the jobs are. On a more flexible and perhaps more contemporary note, however, this study also confirms that going back to school has a substantial payoff in terms of wage growth and movement into more responsible jobs. It suggests that those who do not initially approach the labor market with advantageous human capital can obtain it and reap the projected benefits.

Notes

1. The spiral pattern is to some extent an amalgamation of linear and steady state and requires a very long time frame to observe. Therefore, it will not be examined here. Rather, the three patterns that can be more precisely identified will be the focus: linear, steady state, and transitory.

2. Characteristics of 1966 survey week job (time t) are compared with those for the 1967 survey week job (time $t + 1$). If 1967 data are invalid, then 1968 survey week information is used as the $t + 1$ period to complete the comparison. But no comparison involving a skip of more than one survey year was used. This comparison is then classified according to the criteria given in the text as being either linear, steady state, or transitory. Then, 1967 job characteristics become the period t data and are compared with 1968 job characteristics as the $t + 1$ period, and so on to the 1980 to 1981 comparison.

3. The average wage increase used as the baseline for comparisons represents the annual aggregate increase in median hourly wages over the relevant time period for male wage and salary workers of all ages. These figures are based on CPS data and were calculated from table C19 of U.S. Department of Labor (1982). The occupation

characteristics Data, People, Things, and Intelligence (DPTI) are fourth edition *Dictionary of Occupational Titles* (DOT) attributes of occupations assigned to three-digit Census occupations by taking a weighted average across constituent DOT occupations. The items are complexity in dealing with data (coded on a seven-point scale), with people (coded on an eight-point scale), and with things (coded on an eight-point scale), and amount of intelligence or general learning ability required (coded on a five-point scale). These items were first transformed to a similar metric and then summed to create an aggregate score for each respondent at each survey year. The aggregate score is held to represent overall level in a job hierarchy. For suggestions on using DOT data in social research, see Cain and Treiman (1981).

4. The following formula is used in constructing the wage growth variable:

$$\left[\frac{1981 \text{ wage}}{t_1 \text{ wage}} \right]^a - 1,$$

where t_1 wage = wage in the first survey year in which the respondent was employed and not enrolled, and

$$a = \frac{1}{\text{elapsed years}}$$

5. The Rotter scale consists of 11 items on attitude and motivation. Responses range from 1 to 4 with the lower response indicating a greater sense of internal control, interpreted to reflect initiative (Andrisani, 1977). This variable was created using only the four items which tap individual initiative. The other items concern what happens to workers in general. For a more detailed discussion of the Rotter scale, see Andrisani and Nestel (1975).

6. This percentage is based on comparing employers from one survey year to the next. For those who made more than one employer change between survey years, the percentage of employer changes is undercounted.

References

Andrisani, P.J. 1977. "Internal-External Attitudes, Personal Initiative and the Labor Market Experience of Black and White Men." *Journal of Human Resources 12:* 308–328.

——— and G. Nestel. 1975. "Internal-External Control and Labor Market Experience." In *The Pre-Retirement Years,* Vol. 4, U.S. Department of Labor, Manpower Research, Monograph no. 15. Washington, D.C.: U.S. Government Printing Office.

Beck, E.M., P.M. Horan, and C.M. Tolbert. 1978. "Stratification in a Dual Economy: A Sectoral Model of Earnings Determination." *American Sociological Review 43:*704–720.

Becker, G.S. 1975. *Human Capital,* 2nd ed. New York: Columbia University Press.

Bibb, R., and W. Form. 1977. "The Effects of Industrial, Occupational and Sex Stratification on Wages in Blue Collar Markets." *Social Forces 55:*974–996.

Blau, R.M., and O.D. Duncan. 1967. *The American Occupational Structure.* New York: Wiley.

Cain, Pamela, and Donald Treiman. 1981. "The DOT as a Source of Occupational Data." *American Sociological Review* 46 (June):253–278.

Clawson, Dan. 1980. *Bureaucracy and the Labor Process: The Transformation of U.S. Industry, 1860–1920.* New York: Monthly Review Press.

D'Amico, R.J. 1985. "The Effects of Career Origins on Subsequent Socioeconomic Attainments." *Work and Occupations* 12:3 (August).

Diamond, A.M., Jr. 1983. "The Distribution and Determinants of Individual Wage Profile Slopes." Columbus, Ohio: Center for Human Resource Research.

Doeringer, P., and M. Piore. 1971. *Internal Labor Markets and Manpower Analysis.* Lexington, Mass.: Lexington Books.

Driver, M.J. 1983. "Career Concepts: A New Approach to Career Research." In Ralph Katz, ed., *Career Issues in Human Resource Management.* Englewood Cliffs, N.J.: Prentice-Hall.

Duncan, G.J. 1979. "An Empirical Model of Wage Growth." In Greg J. Duncan and James N. Morgan, eds., *Five Thousand American Families—Patterns of Economic Progress,* Vol. VII. Ann Arbor, Mich.: Institute for Social Research.

Duncan, O.D. 1961. "A Socioeconomic Index for All Occupations." In A.J. Reiss et al., eds., *Occupations and Social Status.* New York: Free Press.

Edwards, R. 1975. "The Social Relations of Production in the Firm and Labor Market Structure." In Edwards, Reich, and Gordon, eds., *Labor Market Segmentation.* Lexington, Mass.: Lexington Books.

Featherman, D.L. 1971. "A Social Structure Model for the Socioeconomic Career." *American Journal of Sociology* 77:293–304.

Felmlee, Diane H. 1982. "Women's Job Mobility Processes within and between Employers." *American Sociological Review* 47:147–151.

Grandjean, B. 1981. "History and Career in a Bureaucratic Labor Market." *American Journal of Sociology* 86:1057–1092.

Hall, D.T. 1976. *Careers in Organizations.* Pacific Palisades, Calif.: Goodyear.

Jacobs, J. 1983. "Industrial Sector and Career Mobility Reconsidered." *American Sociological Review* 48:415–421.

Kalleberg, A.L., and P.M. Hudis. 1979. "Wage Change in Late Career: A Model for the Outcomes of Job Sequences." *Social Science Research* 8:16–40.

Latack, J.C., and L.B. Shaw. 1983. "Routes to Higher Wages among Women Workers: An Analysis of Career Mobility." Columbus, Ohio: Center for Human Resource Research.

Lazear, Edward. 1976. "Age, Experience and Wage Growth." *American Economic Review* 66:548–558.

———. 1979. "The Narrowing of Black-White Wage Differentials Is Illusory." *American Economic Review* 69:553–564.

Lyon, L., and H. Rector-Owen. 1981. "Labor Market Mobility among Young Black and White Women: Longitudinal Models of Occupational Prestige and Income." *Social Science Quarterly* 62:64–78.

Mincer, J. 1970. "The Distribution of Labor Income: A Survey with Special Reference to the Human Capital Approach." *Journal of Economic Literature* 8:1–26.

Raelin, J.A. 1980. *Building a Career: The Effect of Initial Job Experiences and*

Related Work Attitudes on Later Employment. Kalamazoo, Mich.: Upjohn Institute for Employment Research.

Rosenbaum, J. 1979. "Organizational Career Mobility: Promotion Chances in a Corporation during Periods of Growth and Contraction." *American Journal of Sociology 85:* 21–48.

Rosenfeld, R.H. 1980. "Race and Sex Differences in Career Dynamics." *American Sociological Review 45:* 583–609.

Rotter, J.B. 1966. "Generalized Expectancies for Internal vs. External Control of Reinforcement." *Psychological Monographs 80* (Whole no. 609).

Spilerman, S. 1977. "Careers, Labor Market Structure and Socioeconomic Achievement." *American Journal of Sociology 83:* 551–593.

Super, D. 1957. *The Psychology of Careers: An Introduction to Vocational Development.* New York: Harper & Row.

Treas, J., and A. Tyree. 1979. "Prestige versus Socioeconomic Status in The Attainment Processes of American Men and Women." *Social Science Research 8* (no. 3): 201–221.

U.S. Bureau of the Census. 1960. *Census of Population, Alphabetical Index of Occupations and Industries (Revised Edition),* Washington, D.C.: U.S. Government Printing Office.

U.S. Department of Labor, Bureau of Labor Statistics. 1982. *Labor Force Statistics Derived from the Current Population Survey: A Databook,* Vol. 1. Washington, D.C.: U.S. Government Printing Office, September.

Vroom, V.H. 1964. *Work and Motivation.* New York: John Wiley & Sons.

7
Long-Run Effects of Military Service during the Vietnam War

John L. Jackson

A central tenet of human capital theory is that individuals generally invest in schooling and training during their younger years.[1] However, the Vietnam War altered the investment decisions of many young men who reached adulthood in the late 1960s. Some young men who served in the military during this era, hereafter referred to as *veterans,* did so at the expense of work or schooling and were forced to substitute military training for desired civilian training. Conversely, some veterans received training in the military in which they otherwise would not have invested.[2]

While the Vietnam War had a direct impact on the human capital investments of those who served in the military, it also affected the investment decisions of many youths who did not serve, hereafter referred to as *civilians.* The draft system used by the armed forces in this period exempted from service individuals who worked in certain occupations or who met specific school enrollment or hardship qualifications.[3] Thus, by engaging in certain activities that were not necessarily their first choice or optimal choice, young men could avoid military duty.

It is clear that the Vietnam War affected the human capital investments of many young men, but the influence of the conflict on their later labor market performance is unclear. For example, veterans who received military training that was applicable in the civilian sector may have been helped by their service time; veterans whose schooling and work plans were disrupted by service, on the other hand, may have had their performance adversely affected by military service.[4] In addition, service during this time may have imparted certain credentials to veterans that act as a signal to potential civilian employers.[5] This signal may be positive (DeTray, 1982) or negative (Berger and Hirsch, 1983).

Likewise, the Vietnam War may have helped or hindered the labor market performance of civilians. Inasmuch as some individuals upgraded their schooling plans to gain an educational exemption from military duty, the conflict had a positive impact on the performance of civilians. However, civilians who curtailed their schooling or engaged in nonoptimal activities to avoid service might have been subsequently hurt in the labor market.[6]

This study uses data from the Young Men's Cohort of the National Longitudinal Surveys (NLS) of Labor Market Experience to determine what effect the Vietnam War had on the labor market performance of young men age 14 to 19 in 1966. The results indicate that on the whole, service in the military during the Vietnam War had little impact on the long-run labor market performance of this age group of young men. However, there is some variation across race and ability level. Whatever impact service time has on performance seems to be attributable to the credentials effect.

The longitudinal nature of the data makes this investigation unique in several respects. First, various performance measures are employed. In previous analyses, the most popular performance measure used has been wages. However, individuals who do not report earnings are excluded from any analysis using wages as the performance criteria. If the group that does not report earnings has characteristics vastly different from the group reporting wages, then an analysis of earnings differences produces misleading results.[7] An alternative measure of performance, based on the extensive employment history available in the NLS, is the percentage of time an individual is employed. This measure can be used for those who do not report wages as well as for those who do, and is especially useful in analyzing individuals who have unstable employment. The panel data used here also allow analysis in several time frames, so that the effect of military service on both short-run and long-run performance can be determined.

Development

The basic human capital model holds that *Education* and *Experience* are the prime determinants of earnings.[8] Generalizing somewhat, the model posits that labor market performance is a function of *Education, Experience,* and other individual and job-specific characteristics.

The Vietnam War and the draft system may have had direct or indirect impact on the later labor market performance of young men. Inasmuch as military service imparts credentials, either positive or negative, or affects a person's mental or physical health, then the effect is direct. The indirect effect works through the factors that influence performance. That is, an indirect impact of military service on labor market performance is carried through certain determinants of performance like *Education* and *Experience* which themselves can be a function of military service.[9]

A more complete model of labor market performance accounts for the possible direct and indirect effects of military duty. In this three-equation recursive model, where *Education* and *Experience* as well as labor market performance are functions of service time,[10] military service and individual characteristics influence the amount of schooling a young man gains. His schooling, individual characteristics, and military service, in turn, influence the amount of work experience he accumulates, and all of these variables affect labor market outcomes.

Individual characteristics like parental education are expected to have a positive impact on schooling, while certain locational variables should have a negative effect. Although a positive relationship between military service and education might exist for veterans who use their G.I. benefits, service time is expected to cause a disruption in the schooling plans of the majority of veterans.

Because schooling is likely to increase a person's marketability and work attachment, a positive relationship is expected between *Education* and *Experience*. Certain socioeconomic background variables should positively affect experience, while locational variables such as local unemployment rates should have a negative impact. Some veterans may have received military training that would increase their marketability or work attachment, but military service probably interrupted work experience for most veterans.

It is widely accepted that *Education* and *Experience* have a positive effect on labor market performance. Some of the individual and job-specific variables also expected to positively influence performance include *Parental Education, Non-South* and *SMSA Residency, Union Membership, Firm Size,* and employment in certain occupations and industries. After controlling for any indirect effects, military service should have a positive direct influence on labor market performance. This influence reflects the impact of credentials or training gained from service.

Because of their higher rate of return, individuals of higher ability would optimally invest in more human capital than their less talented counterparts.[11] However, all individuals receive similar amounts of training in the military regardless of their ability.[12] It is likely, then, that military service restricts the human capital investment of individuals of high ability while it increases the investment of people of low ability. The model is therefore modified further by adding *Ability* as another variable affecting labor market outcomes.

Data

To form the universe for this analysis, two restrictions are imposed on the Young Men's Cohort.[13] First, only those individuals who were interviewed in 1981 are included in the universe, ensuring that a long-run investigation can be made.[14] The second restriction limits the analysis to persons 14 to 19 years of age as of the 1966 interview. NLS respondents older than age 19 eligible for military service, and if already serving in 1966, were excluded from the NLS sample. This type of sample selection bias did not occur for NLS respondents age 14–19 in 1966, since they were age ineligible for military duty.[15]

The 2,289 individuals in this universe—560 blacks and 1,729 whites—are grouped into two categories, veterans and civilians.[16] Members of the universe who joined the military anytime after the 1966 interview and separated from the service by the 1976 interview are considered veterans.[17] The civilian group consists of those in the universe who never served in the military.[18]

As shown in table 7–1, roughly one-third of the universe served in the military. Among these veterans, about 41 percent of blacks and 26 percent of whites were drafted into service; whereas 38 percent of whites served in the navy or air force, only 24 percent of blacks served in these "high-technology" branches.

Three performance measures are used in this analysis. The 1976 wage rate is considered a short-run performance gauge because it reflects relative earnings, before a large amount of firm-specific human capital is amassed. Earnings 5 years later (1981 wages) are indicative of labor market performance after the adjustment from school or military to work is made. This long-run measure also allows for wage changes so that any spurious short-run influences can be resolved. The final measure, percentage of time employed between the start of the first postschool or military job and the 1981 interview date, is also considered to be a long-run gauge of performance. This measure reflects not only the employability of an individual, but also the stability of employment and thus is particularly useful in analyzing the performance of a group in which a sporadic work history is probable.

These performance measures, along with other characteristics, are presented in table 7–2. Despite some variation across race and ability level, the performance measures of veterans and civilians are similar. In particular, there is no statistically significant difference between the 1976 wages of veterans and civilians in the universe, a finding that holds true for both blacks and whites and within specific levels of ability. Comparison of 1981 wages between the two service groups also shows little overall difference. However, there is some evidence, especially among whites, that military service helps the performance of low-ability individuals and hurts that of high ability persons in the long run.

Regardless of ability and race, military duty has a positive impact on the percentage of time an individual is employed. That is, veterans have a higher percentage of work time than their civilian counterparts, though the difference is significant only among whites. This indicates that after a period of

Table 7–1
Sample Sizes by Race and Military Status, and Percentage Distribution of Veterans across Entry Status and Branch

	Total	Black	White
Total sample[a]	2,289 (10,563)	560 (1,159)	1,729 (9,405)
Civilians	1,561 (7,088)	392 (787)	1,169 (6,301)
Veterans	728 (3,476)	168 (372)	560 (3,104)
Entry status (%)[b]			
Drafted	27.6	40.6	26.1
Enlisted	61.9	56.2	62.6
OCS/ROTC	3.1	3.3	3.1
Other	7.4	0.0	8.2
Branch of Service (%)[b]			
Army	56.4	59.8	56.0
Navy	18.9	6.9	20.3
Air force	13.7	16.8	13.3
Marine corps	10.5	16.5	9.8

Note: Universe consisted of young men age 14–19 in 1966 who were interviewed in 1981.
[a]Sample sizes multiplied by a weighting factor to approximate the general population are presented in parentheses.
[b]Distributions based on weighted sample sizes.

adjusting to the labor market, veterans have a stronger work commitment than do civilians.

Somewhat surprisingly, there is little difference in adjustment time between veterans and civilians. The amount of time between leaving school or the military and starting a job is similar for veterans and civilians regardless of race and ability level.[19] Comparison of other characteristics between the two groups shows that among blacks, veterans have more education in 1981, are less likely to live in the South, have less experience and are more likely to belong to a labor union than are civilians. White veterans, compared to their civilian counterparts, have less schooling and a lower parental education level, have less experience, and work for a larger size company. These differences indicate general relationships between background, military service, and performance; the next section will identify more specifically the exact effect background and service time have on labor market performance.

Table 7-2
Mean Values of Selected Characteristics of Civilians and Veterans, by Race and Ability Level[a]

| | Blacks | | | | | | Whites | | | | | |
| | Civilians | | | Veterans | | | Civilians | | | Veterans | | |
	Total	LO	HI	Total	LO	HI	Total	LO	HI	Total	LO	HI
Performance												
Wage 1976 (1976 dollars)	4.55 (0.17)[b]	3.84 (0.39)	5.35 (0.96)	4.58	3.73	4.99	5.66 (0.16)	5.07 (0.76)	6.47 (1.03)	5.64	5.23	6.22
Wage 1981 (1981 dollars)	7.26 (0.58)	6.03 (1.07)	8.62+ (1.82)	7.08	6.62	7.36	9.80 (0.39)	8.78 (1.17)	11.38 (0.36)	9.89	9.24	10.94
Percentage time worked[c]	82.78 (1.15)	82.28 (0.55)	83.01 (1.23)	84.87	84.02	86.93	87.86* (2.21)	86.53 (0.57)	90.86 (0.31)	89.71	87.47	91.28
Background												
Parental education[d]	9.26 (0.21)	7.34* (2.81)	10.44 (0.74)	9.19	8.85	10.00	11.98* (3.27)	11.08+ (1.80)	12.80* (2.25)	11.49	10.55	12.22
Labor market adjustment[e]	4.63 (0.36)	3.30 (0.10)	6.34 (0.65)	4.29	3.42	4.85	2.92 (0.23)	3.00 (0.17)	2.76 (0.18)	2.84	3.12	2.65
Education-1981[f]	12.64 (1.52)	10.84* (4.22)	14.00 (0.63)	12.96	12.49	13.75	14.14* (5.43)	12.73 (0.20)	15.17* (4.77)	13.51	12.77	14.22
South-1981[g]	0.65 (1.55)	0.74* (2.14)	0.51 (0)	0.58	0.55	0.51	0.32 (1.27)	0.38* (2.68)	0.30 (0.45)	0.29	0.26	0.32

Experience-1981[h]	92.60* (6.35)	114.82 (3.47)	78.98 (2.15)	63.43	82.80	61.35	81.17* (3.37)	91.93 (2.86)	74.71 (0.27)	72.16	77.77	73.38
Firm size-1981[i]	1.86 (0.88)	1.83 (1.53)	1.82 (0.91)	1.96	1.53	2.01	1.81* (2.90)	1.89 (0.43)	1.71* (2.08)	1.99	2.01	2.10
Union-membership[j]	0.22* (3.05)	0.18 (1.49)	0.29 (1.03)	0.35	0.30	0.37	0.20 (0.93)	0.25 (0.92)	0.15 (0.56)	0.22	0.29	0.17

Note: Universe consisted of young men aged 14–19 in 1966 who were interviewed in 1981.

[a] Individuals are grouped into one of three ability groups. The "LO" ability group consists of individuals scoring more than one-half a standard deviation below the race-specific mean on the KOWW test, while the "HI" ability group consists of those whose KOWW score is more than one-half a standard deviation above the mean. Individuals whose KOWW score lies within a half-standard deviation of the race-specific mean are in the "MID" ability group.

[b] t-statistics in parentheses. Computed as $\dfrac{\bar{m}^c - \bar{m}^v}{(v^c/n^c + v^v/n^v)^{1/2}}$ where $\bar{m}$, V, and n represent the mean, variance, and sample size of each characteristic for civilians and veterans (superscript c and v). This statistic measures significance of difference between civilians and veterans within given race and ability groups.

[c] Percentage of time worked between the first postschool/military job and the 1981 interview.

[d] Educational attainment of parent with the most schooling, measured in 1966.

[e] Number of months between leaving school/military and starting the first postschool/military job.

[f] Highest grade of education completed as of 1981 interview.

[g] Dichotomous variable equal to 1 if respondent lived in South in 1981, 0 otherwise.

[h] Number of months worked between leaving school and the 1981 interview.

[i] Scale measure of number of employees at respondent's work setting; 1 = less than 25 employees; 2 = 25 to 99; 3 = 100 to 499; 4 = 500 to 999; and 5 = 1,000 and more.

[j] Dichotomous variable equal to 1 if respondent was a member of a union in 1981, 0 otherwise.

+ Significant at .10 level, two-tail t-test.
* Significant at .05 level, two-tail t-test.

Results

The three equations forming the model in this analysis should be viewed as reduced-form equations because the identification problem prevents estimation of the structural model. The intent of this analysis is to determine the effect of military service on subsequent civilian labor market performance; for this reason only the reduced-form performance equations are estimated, although various measures of performance are utilized.

As mentioned earlier, wages in 1976 are used as a short-run measure of performance. Hourly earnings in 1981 represent one long-run aspect of performance, and percentage of time worked between leaving school or the military and the 1981 survey (*Worktime*) is used as another long-run measure. Because the labor market experience of blacks differs from that of whites, the performance equations are estimated separately for each race group.[20] The equations using wages as the dependent variable are in a semilogarithmic form. [21]

Table 7–3 presents the results of the estimation using 1976 wages as the measure of performance. Several findings hold for both blacks and whites across various specifications. As expected, both education and experience are significant positive determinants of earnings. Ability, as measured by the Knowledge of the World of Work (KOWW) score, also had a strong positive impact on 1976 wages. All else constant, living in a Standard Metropolitan Statistical Area (SMSA) increased earnings by 14 to 15 percent, while having a health problem decreased earnings 8 to 9 percent.

Certain job-specific characteristics were also significant in determining 1976 wages. Earnings were found to be positively correlated with firm size and union membership. Workers in the agricultural, trade, and public service sectors earned less than those in the mining, manufacturing and construction industries. Similarly, workers in clerical, farm, and service occupations earned less than their counterparts who were craftsmen or operatives.

While there is no evidence that military service affects the performance of blacks, various results indicate that service has an impact on the performance of whites.[22] The estimated coefficient on the dichotomous variable denoting military duty is significant and positive across several specifications. Again, there appears to be an interaction between service and ability such that high-ability individuals are hurt by the military duty while low-ability individuals are helped.

The positive short-run effects of military duty experienced by whites are likely due to the credentials conferred on veterans by their service. That is, as shown in the last specification in table 7–3, *Military Experience* (time in the service) has a negative impact on performance while the dichotomous variable denoting service is positive. Thus, service has a positive impact on performance despite the fact that military training is not highly valued in the short run by civilian employers.

As shown in table 7–4, use of 1981 wages as the performance measure results in similar findings. *Education, Experience,* and *Ability* are all positive determinants of earnings, as are *Firm Size, Union Membership,* and *SMSA Residency.* Negative influences include having a health problem, working as a clerk, laborer, or farmer, and being employed in the agricultural, trade, or service industries. Having a health problem has a negative impact only for whites.

The 1981 wage equation includes a variable that accounts for the adjustment between school or the military and civilian work. This variable may capture certain unmeasurable aspects of a person's employability or proxy for the person's reservation wage adjustment process.[23] Regardless, the adjustment period is expected to affect long-run performance negatively, a result found to hold among whites.

Again, the coefficients on the military variables are significant only for whites.[24] The negative coefficient on the interaction of service and KOWW signifies that military duty is especially helpful to the long-run performance of low-ability individuals. The long-run aspect of the analysis and the detailed work history allow the experience variable to be divided into three segments: preservice civilian experience, military experience (time in the military), and postservice civilian experience.[25] The final specification in table 7–4 indicates that, due to deterioration or nontransferability of training neither preservice civilian experience nor military experience is rewarded in the labor market. Thus, the positive impact of military service on long-run performance is most likely due to credentials effects or signaling.

The estimated results of the performance equations having *Worktime* as the dependent variable are presented in table 7–5. The variables used to identify the variation in *Worktime* deserve some explanation. Because *Worktime* is defined as the percentage of time spent working between the beginning of the first postschool or postmilitary job and the 1981 interview, the four basic explanatory variables—*Education, Age* (to proxy for experience), *Health Status,* and *Residence in the South*—are measured just prior to the start of the job. In addition, several variables are used to denote a change in education, residence, and work environment between the start of the job and the 1981 survey. Finally, an adjustment variable is included because individuals who experienced difficulty in finding a job are considered less marketable and are expected to have a number of nonwork intervals.

The results show that the long-run employment performance of both blacks and whites is negatively affected by the length of time between leaving school or the military and starting a job. Education positively affects *Worktime,* while having a health problem has a negative impact. Changes over time that positively affect performance include an increase in firm size and movement out of an SMSA area. Military service seems to be related to less stable employment patterns for whites and blacks, but particularly for blacks. The impact of military service on *Worktime* is negative and significant

Table 7–3
OLS Estimates of the Determinants of 1976 Wages, by Race

Independent Variables	Blacks			Whites		
Education[a]	0.0273*	0.0258*	0.0259*	0.0408*	0.0416*	0.0382*
	(2.87)	(2.68)	(2.69)	(6.82)	(6.79)	(6.26)
Health[b]	−0.0932	−0.0949	−0.0958	−0.0806*	−0.0753+	−0.0795*
	(−1.54)	(−1.57)	(−1.58)	(−2.04)	(−1.90)	(−2.00)
SMSA[c]	0.1471*	0.1505*	0.1517*	0.1406*	0.1427*	0.1382*
	(3.66)	(3.72)	(3.74)	(6.19)	(6.29)	(6.08)
Experience[d]	0.0011*	0.0012*	0.0012+	0.0019*	0.0021*	0.0020*
	(2.12)	(1.96)	(1.90)	(6.16)	(6.40)	(5.25)
Occupation[e]						
Labor	−0.1456*	−0.1434*	−0.1433*	−0.0419	−0.0378	−0.0508
Clerk	−0.1175*	−0.1258*	−0.1246*	−0.1345*	−0.1342*	−0.1370*
Professional	0.0702	0.0794	0.0785	0.0335	0.0400	0.0362
Manager	0.1743+	0.1804+	0.1785+	0.0092	0.0097	0.0083
Other	−0.1575*	−0.1623*	−0.1639*	−0.1373	−0.1337*	−0.1447*
Industry[f]						
Agriculture	−0.4330*	−0.4267*	−0.4245*	−0.3539*	−0.3508*	−0.3497*
Transportation	0.0064	0.0092	0.0099	−0.0244	−0.0232	−0.0104
Trade	−0.1361*	−0.1387*	−0.1360*	−0.1741*	−0.1717*	−0.1712*
Finance/Insurance	−0.1717+	−0.1721+	−0.1687	0.0268	0.0310	0.0240
Service	−0.0888	−0.0762	−0.0769	−0.1521*	−0.1542*	−0.1388*
Public service	−0.1512*	−0.1447*	−0.1415*	−0.2805*	−0.2799*	−0.2781*
Firm size[g]	0.0519*	0.0516*	0.0519*	0.0338*	0.0336*	0.0345*
	(3.83)	(3.81)	(3.82)	(3.77)	(3.75)	(3.85)
Union membership[h]	0.2329*	0.2357*	0.2367*	0.1790	0.1790	0.1779*
	(5.92)	(6.00)	(6.01)	(7.13)	(7.13)	(7.07)

Ability[i]	0.0075* (3.05)	0.0073* (2.95)	0.0065* (2.25)	0.0098* (6.56)	0.0115* (6.45)	0.0119* (6.68)
Military[j]		0.1068 (1.62)	0.0425 (0.30)		0.2225* (2.17)	0.3589* (3.34)
Military *KOWW[k]		−0.0016 (−1.03)	0.0024 (0.52)		−0.0056+ (−1.87)	−0.0057+ (−1.89)
Military Experience[l]			−0.0017 (−1.08)			−0.0027* (−2.67)
Constant	5.2586*	5.2613*	5.2778*	5.1782*	5.0912*	5.1320*
$\bar{R}^2$	0.4325	0.4302	0.4290	0.2844	0.2868	0.2829
N	375	375	375	1,232	1,232	1,232

(t-statistics in parentheses.)

Note: Universe consisted of young men aged 14 to 19 in 1966 who were interviewed in 1981.

[a]Highest grade completed as of 1976 interview.

[b]Dichotomous variable equal to 1 if respondent had health problem in 1976, 0 otherwise.

[c]Dichotomous variable equal to 1 if respondent lived in an SMSA in 1976, 0 otherwise.

[d]Number of months worked between leaving school and the 1976 interview.

[e]Dichotomous variables equal to 1 if respondent's occupation in 1976 was that listed, 0 otherwise. Omitted category is craftsmen/operatives.

[f]Dichotomous variables equal to 1 if respondent worked in given industry in 1976, 0 otherwise. Omitted category is mining/manufacturing/construction.

[g]Firm size in 1976. Scale measure with 1 = less than 25; 2 = 25 to 99; 3 = 100 to 499; 4 = 500 to 999; 5 = 1,000 and over.

[h]Dichotomous variable equal to 1 if respondent was a member of a union in 1976, 0 otherwise.

[i]Ability as proxied by KOWW score.

[j]Dichotomous variable equal to 1 if respondent is in the veteran group, 0 otherwise.

[k]Interaction term equal to the product of the military dichotomous variable and the KOWW score.

[l]Months of military experience, equal to zero for civilians.

+ Significant at the .10 level, two-tail t-test.

* Significant at the .05 level, two-tail t-test.

Table 7–4
OLS Estimates of the Determinants of 1981 Wages, by Race

Independent variables	Blacks			Whites		
Education[a]	0.0433* (4.16)	0.0435* (4.18)	0.0437* (4.19)	0.0563* (9.04)	0.0556* (8.80)	0.0545* (8.66)
SMSA residency[b]	0.1529* (3.68)	0.1496* (3.60)	0.1508* (3.62)	0.1593* (6.56)	0.1619* (6.66)	0.1605* (6.60)
Health[c]	-0.0289 (-0.39)	-0.0245 (-0.33)	-0.0230 (-0.31)	-0.1114* (-2.88)	-0.1084* (-2.80)	-0.1093* (-2.81)
Firm size[d]	0.0662* (4.25)	0.0666* (4.28)	0.0652* (4.16)	0.0498* (5.38)	0.0498* (5.37)	0.0501* (5.37)
Union membership[e]	0.2405* (5.62)	0.2378* (5.55)	0.2386* (5.58)	0.1710* (6.43)	0.1699* (6.39)	0.1706* (6.40)
Ability[f]	0.0039 (1.49)	0.0037 (1.41)	0.0042 (1.36)	0.0083* (5.18)	0.0103* (5.31)	0.0105* (5.39)
Occupation[g]						
Labor	-0.1574*	-0.1569*	-0.1559*	-0.1414*	-0.1439*	-0.1446*
Clerk	-0.2101*	-0.2017*	-0.1996*	-0.0895*	-0.0867*	-0.0907*
Professional	0.2056*	0.2121*	0.2098*	0.0331	0.0399	0.0404
Manager	0.2165*	0.2234*	0.2335*	0.0929*	0.0943*	0.0948*
Other	-0.1496*	-0.1553*	-0.1544*	-0.2214*	-0.2183*	-0.2198*
Industry[h]						
Agriculture	-0.2583*	-0.2479*	-0.2370+	-0.3907*	-0.3806*	-0.3821*
Transportation	0.0752	0.0781	0.0563	0.0315	0.0283	0.0305
Trade	-0.1952*	-0.1932*	-0.1915*	-0.1470*	-0.1473*	-0.1442*
Finance/insurance	-0.1740	-0.1660	-0.1734	0.0433	0.0458	0.0476
Service	-0.2137*	-0.2072*	-0.1951*	-0.0822+	-0.0876*	-0.0891+
Public service	-0.1158	-0.1115	-0.0997	-0.3171*	-0.3196*	-0.3222*
Public administration	-0.0242	-0.0220	-0.0332	-0.0186	-0.0245	-0.0265

Experience[i]	0.0012*	0.0013*	0.0013*	0.0009*	0.0010*	0.0008*
	(2.84)	(3.04)	(2.57)	(3.74)	(3.85)	(2.83)
Adjustment[j]	0.0009	0.0009	0.0008	−0.0041*	−0.0042*	−0.0041*
	(0.39)	(0.39)	(0.35)	(−2.13)	(−2.14)	(−2.12)
Military						
Military[k]	0.0442	0.0442	0.0188		0.2149*	0.2306*
Military KOWW[l]			−0.0023		−0.0060+	−0.0063*
Premilitary experience[m]			−0.0010			−0.0002
Military experience[n]			0.0026			−0.0003
Postmilitary experience[p]			0.0021*			0.0010*
Constant	5.4996*	5.4733*	5.4563*	5.5014*	5.4327*	5.4520*
R̄²	0.4423	0.4425	0.4439	0.3283	0.3296	0.3270

(t-statistics in parentheses.)

Note: Universe consisted of young men aged 14 to 19 in 1966 who were interviewed in 1981. Sample sizes equal for 389 blacks, 1,155 for whites.

[a] Highest grade of school completed as of 1981 interview.

[b] Dichotomous variable equal to 1 if residence in 1981 is in SMSA, 0 otherwise.

[c] Dichotomous variable equal to 1 if respondent had health problem in 1981, 0 otherwise.

[d] Scale measure of firm size in 1981, where 1 = less than 25 employees, 2 = 25 to 99, 3 = 100 to 499, 4 = 500 to 999, and 5 = 1,000 and more.

[e] Dichotomous variable equal to 1 if member of union in 1981, 0 otherwise.

[f] KOWW score.

[g] Dichotomous variables equal to 1 if 1981 occupation is as listed, 0 otherwise. Omitted category is craftsmen/operatives.

[h] Dichotomous variables equal to 1 if 1981 industry is as listed, 0 otherwise. Omitted category is mining, manufacturing, and construction.

[i] Number of months worked between leaving school and the 1981 interview. (Equal to 0 for veterans in specification 3.)

[j] Number of months between leaving school or the military and starting the first postschool/military job.

[k] Dichotomous variable equal to 1 if respondent is in the veteran group, 0 otherwise.

[l] Interaction term equal to the product of the dichotomous military variable and the KOWW score.

[m] Premilitary experience equal to the number of months between leaving school and starting service for veterans, 0 for civilians.

[n] Military experience equal to the number of months spent in the service for veterans, 0 for civilians.

[p] Postmilitary experience equal to the number of months worked between leaving the military and the 1981 interview for veterans, 0 for civilians.

+ Significant at the .10 level, two-tail t-test.

* Significant at the .05 level, two-tail t-test.

Table 7–5
OLS Estimates of the Determinants of Worktime, by Race

	Blacks		Whites	
Education[a]	1.1900+	.9204	.6902+	.5123+
	(1.94)	(1.46)	(2.55)	(1.72)
Age[a]	.2326	.7297	.7199*	.8875*
	(0.53)	(1.35)	(3.53)	(3.76)
Health status[a]	−7.1218	−7.3011	−4.5124*	−4.7606*
	(−1.59)	(−1.64)	(−2.89)	(−3.03)
Residence in the South[a]	9.953*	9.5177*	.7588	.6459
	(3.81)	(3.64)	(0.71)	(0.60)
Change in education[b]	2.0279	1.1427	1.7414	1.5195
	(0.73)	(0.41)	(1.30)	(1.12)
Adjustment[c]	−.5209*	−.5292*	−1.3507*	−1.3535*
	(−2.31)	(−2.35)	(−13.8)	(−13.84)
Moved south to north[d]	2.9322	2.7624	4.1842	4.3253
	(0.60)	(0.57)	(1.38)	(1.42)
Moved north to south[e]	−2.0050	−2.8559	−1.2580	−1.4886
	(−0.28)	(−0.40)	(−0.53)	(−0.62)
Urban-rural[f]	−13.1866	−11.8427	−5.5243+	−5.3962+
	(−1.23)	(−1.11)	(−1.88)	(−1.83)
Rural-urban[g]	−1.9381	−1.4216	.3719	.5683
	(−0.47)	(−0.35)	(0.19)	(0.29)
Union-nonunion[h]	7.4816+	7.6261+	−2.0745	−2.0726
	(1.89)	(1.94)	(−1.06)	(−1.06)
Nonunion-union[i]	1.2634	1.2415	−6.8056*	−6.8689*
	(0.37)	(0.36)	(−3.69)	(−3.72)
Change in firm size[j]	4.07*	4.2877*	2.8055*	2.8534*
	(2.70)	(2.85)	(4.00)	(4.07)
Military[k]		−5.5471+		−1.7096
		(−1.79)		(−1.41)
Constant	50.9986*	45.6492*	63.7542*	63.0306*
$\bar{R}^2$	.1221	.1298	.2259	.2273

(*t*-statistics in parentheses.)
Note: Universe consisted of young men aged 14 to 19 in 1966 who were interviewed in 1981. Sample size equals 392 for blacks, 1,171 for whites.
[a]Variable (see text) measured as of end of school or military.
[b]Dichotomous variable equal to 1 if received more education between start of first postschool/military job and 1981.
[c]Number of months between leaving school or the military and starting the first postschool/military job.
[d]Dichotomous variable equal to 1 if respondent moved from south to north between start of first job after military/school (t_1) and 1981.
[e]Dichotomous variable equal to 1 if respondent moved from north to south between t_1 and 1981.
[f]Dichotomous variable equal to 1 if respondent moved from an urban to a rural (non-SMSA) area between t_1 and 1981.

Table 7–5 continued

gDichotomous variable equal to 1 if respondent moved from a rural (non-SMSA area to an urban area.

hChange from unionized firm in 1976 to nonunionized firm in 1981.

iChange from nonunionized firm in 1976 to unionized firm in 1981.

jChange in firm size, equal to difference between 1976 and 1981 firm-size variables.

kDichotomous variable equal to 1 if respondent is in veteran group, 0 otherwise.

+ Significant at the .10 level, two-tail t-test.

*Significant at the .05 level, two-tail t-test.

for blacks; although it is also negative for whites, the estimated coefficient is not significant.

To better understand how military service affects individuals' long-run labor market performance, a simulation is carried out to determine whether veterans would have performed better had they been civilians, and vice versa. To do this, 1981 wages and *Worktime* are estimated separately for white veterans and civilians.[26] By substituting the characteristics of veterans into the estimated equations for civilians (and vice versa), it can be determined how veterans would have fared as civilians and how civilians would have fared as veterans. In addition this "decomposition analysis" (Blinder, 1973) will reveal whether the performance difference between veterans and civilians is due to differences in the characteristics or market treatments of these two groups.[27]

The results of this simulation, presented in table 7–6, indicate that military service has a small positive effect on long-run performance when performance is measured by wages. That is, veterans are predicted to have 1981 earnings about one percent higher than their civilian counterparts. *Worktime,* however, is virtually the same for veterans and civilians. It is interesting to note that the major impact on 1981 wages comes from civilian-veteran differences in market treatment and the shift coefficient. Differences in background characteristics have very little impact on relative performance.

Previous, analyses using the decomposition approach define "discrimination" as the sum of the effects due to market treatment and the shift coefficient.[28] As table 7–6 shows, the sum of these influences is negative for earnings. That is, if white veterans and civilians had the same shift coefficient and were treated the same in the labor market, then veterans' wages would be about 1 percent lower than that reported. Thus, whatever "discrimination" exists in the civilian market works in favor of veterans, reinforcing the notion that the positive impact of military service on long-run wages is due to signaling or to a positive credentials effect.

Conclusions

The Vietnam conflict affected the work lives of many young men who reached adulthood in the late 1960s. Youths nearing draft-eligible age during

Table 7–6
Accounting for Civilian-Veteran Performance Differentials: Decomposition of Mean 1981 Wages and Worktime

	1981 Wages (%)	Worktime (percentage points)
Total difference[a]	– 1.29	– .002
Subtotal[b]	23.39	– 12.09
Attributable to characteristics[c]	– 0.16	– 1.19
Attributable to treatment[d]	23.58	– 10.86
Shift coefficient[e]	– 20.00	12.09
Discrimination measure[f]	– 1.15	1.22

Note: Universe consisted of white men aged 14 to 19 in 1966 who were interviewed in 1981. Sample size equals 1,155 for 1981 wages, and 1,171 for worktime. Negative sign means advantage for veterans, positive means advantage for civilians. For example, – 20 for the shift coefficient of wages means that if veterans had the same constant term as civilians, their wages would be lower by 20 percent.

[a]Includes shift coefficient: $\sum_{i=0} a_i^c \bar{X}_i^c - \sum_{i=0} a_i^v \bar{X}_i^v$ (includes a logarithmic transformation for 1981 wages).

[b]Does not include the effect of coefficient: $\sum_{i\neq1} a_i^c \bar{X}_i^c - \sum_{i=1} a_i^v \bar{X}_i^v$ (plus a logarithmic transformation for 1981 wages).

[c]Equal to $\sum_{i=1} a_i^c (\bar{X}_i^c - \bar{X}_i^v)$ (plus a logarithmic transformation for 1981 wages).

[d]Equal to $\sum_{i=1} \bar{X}_i^v (a_i^c - a_i^v)$ (plus a logarithmic transformation for 1981 wages).

[e]Equals $a_0^c - a_o^v$ (plus a logarithmic transformation for 1981 wages).

[f]Equal to the sum of the shift coefficient and treatment effects. Note the multiplicative construction for 1981 wages (for example, $-1.15 = ((-.20)*(1.2358) - 1)$).

this era faced a unique set of activities they could pursue, some helpful to long-run performance and others harmful. Military service was one available option, the effect of which is not easily predicted. In fact, the existing literature concerning the effects of military service on subsequent civilian labor market performance is divided.

The analyses showed that veterans and nonveterans have similar background characteristics and as a whole performed similarly in the civilian economy. However, some differences were noted among different racial and ability groups. Military service increased significantly the wages of white veterans, but black veterans did not differ significantly from civilians. White veterans of relatively low ability were helped by their service while high-ability veterans were harmed.

The multivariate analysis suggests that military service imparts positive credentials on veterans that are recognized and rewarded by civilian employers. Our decomposition analysis corroborates this finding. That is, a commonly used measure of "discrimination" shows that veterans receive preferential treatment in the civilian labor market.

In conclusion, the results of this chapter indicate that service in the military during the Vietnam War did not harm the long-run labor market performance of veterans when performance is measured by earnings.[29] In fact, depending on race and ability level, the results indicate that young men might even have been helped by serving. The picture is somewhat different, however, for the amount of time worked after leaving school or the military. Although military service did not significantly affect the proportion of time employed for whites, blacks who served in the military spent significantly less time employed than their civilian counterparts.

Notes

1. The seminal work of Mincer (1974) outlines the basics of human capital theory.

2. In addition, some veterans used GI benefits to obtain schooling they otherwise could not have afforded.

3. In order to maintain the civilian economy, the selective service process granted exemptions to certain "crucial" occupations. In addition, individuals enrolled in a program of higher education, married individuals with dependents, and sole surviving family members were excused from service. (Kohen, et al. 1977; National Advisory Commission on Selective Service, 1967).

4. Norrblum (1976), and Fredland and Little (1980) maintain that service has a positive impact due to the easy transferral of military skills to the civilian sector. Oi (1967), Kassing (1970), and Cutright (1974) attribute the negative effects of military service to career disruptions.

5. The literature on signaling or screening (see Stiglitz, 1975; Wolpin, 1977) holds that human capital investments do not necessarily increase productivity but instead indicate to employers that the individual may become productive. Thus, the minimum physical and mental requirements necessary to serve in the military are the "credentials" imparted to veterans; employers assume all veterans can become at least as productive as individuals with these minimum requirements.

6. To take advantage of certain exemptions, individuals might have gotten married and had children, entered exempt (but nonoptional) occupations, or intentionally harmed their health.

7. This is one aspect of the well-known selectivity problem. See Heckman (1976).

8. Human capital theory has evolved from the works of Mincer (1958) and Houthakker (1959) to the classic pieces of Becker (1964) and Mincer (1974).

9. This section depicts performance as a function of military service. However, the *threat* of possible service had an impact on some individuals who did not serve. Unfortunately, we cannot distinguish between affected and nonaffected civilians; thus the discussion concerns only the effects of actually serving.

10. Since no explicit assumptions regarding the disturbance terms are made, this system is not a true recursive model. Although the model might best be analyzed as a simultaneous system, there is an identification problem, so only the reduced form is estimated. See King and Knapp (1978) and Blinder (1973).

11. Throughout this chapter, "ability" is used to denote innate intelligence. As is common in the literature (see Griliches, 1976; and Griliches and Mason, 1972) and IQ-related measure (here, KOWW) is used to proxy for ability.

12. Preliminary tables using data in the Young Men's Cohort shows that controlling for race, individuals within given branches received similar amounts of training regardless of KOWW level.

13. The cohort of the NLS contains detailed information on the activities over time of an age group of young men. The original (1966) sample consisted of 5,225 young men between the ages of 14 and 24. Though part of this sample was lost to attrition over time, data on 15 years of activity (up to 1981) are currently available for a significant portion of the cohort. Reasons for attrition include refusal to participate in the NLS, failure to locate an individual who moved, and death of a cohort member. Of the original sample 3,591 (or about 69 percent) were interviewed in 1981—2,751 whites and 840 blacks.

14. To increase the sample size, a small number of individuals who were interviewed in 1980 but not in 1981 were included in the universe.

15. In 1966, the selective service system drew people in the age range starting from the top; few 14–19 year olds were seriously threatened by the draft. See National Advisory Commission on Selective Service (1967).

16. Each individual in the NLS is assigned a "weight" equal to the inverse of the probability of being selected. The general population can be approximated by multiplying each observation by this weight variable. Thus, the 2,289 individuals in the universe represent about 10.6 million people in the general population—9.4 million whites and 1.2 million blacks.

17. According to a Veterans Administration publication (1981), the "Vietnam era" is defined as the time between August 1964 and May 1975. In addition, the All Volunteer Force (AVF) was instigated in 1973. Thus, individuals who left the service prior to 1976 were most likely non-AVF Vietnam-era veterans.

18. Because of the draft system used during this era, it is commonly thought that the civilian and veteran groups are vastly different. In particular, due to deferments and minimum military requirements, it is expected that civilians would more often be in the high-ability and the low-ability groups. However, this contention is not supported by our data.

19. Actually, adjustment time is measured as time between leaving school and starting work for both civilians and veterans who received postservice schooling.

20. The Chow-test results in an F-statistic of 11.84, significant at the .99 confidence level, so that the null hypothesis that blacks and whites came from the same population is not accepted.

21. This is the form found to be "best" by Heckman and Polachek (1974).

22. Among blacks, both the t and F statistics on the military variables were non-significant regardless of specification. Among whites, the t-statistics are significant, as is the F-test for the final specification.

23. As the search period continues, an individual will adjust his reservation wage downward.

24. Unfortunately, the F-test shows that the military variables play only a small role in explaining 1981 wages.

25. The measure of experience does not change for civilians. That is, civilians have a value of 0 for all military-related experience variables, and veterans have a value of 0 for the civilian-only experience variable. The applicable experience variable for veterans now becomes postservice civilian experience.

26. The decomposition analysis is restricted to whites since only whites had enough veterans to ensure that an adequate sample size would exist.

27. The mean difference between two groups—here veterans (v) and civilians (c)—can be broken into two parts:

$$\overline{Y}^v - \overline{Y}^c = (a_o^v - a_o^c) + \left(\sum_{i=1}^{n} a_i^v \overline{X}_i^v - \sum_{i=1}^{n} a_i^c \overline{X}_i^c \right).$$

In addition, the latter part, sources explained by the regression, can be broken into a part due to differences in characteristics and a part due to differential treatment:

$$\sum a^v \overline{X}^v - \sum a^c X^c = \sum a^v (X^v - X^c) + \sum X^c (a^v - a^c).$$

28. See Kim and Jackson (1983).

29. Inasmuch as the reason for not being in the sample is related to military service, the results may be biased. This is the selectivity problem alluded to in note 7. Future research might try to account for the bias resulting from noninterview reason, or from the military selection process.

References

Becker, G. 1964. *Human Capital.* New York: National Bureau for Economic Research.

Berger, M., and B. Hirsch. 1983. "Veteran Status as a Screening Device: The Experience of Vietnam-Era Veterans." Lexington: University of Kentucky.

Blinder, A. 1973. "Wage Discrimination: Reduced Form and Structural Estimates." *Journal of Human Resources* 8 (no. 4):436–455.

Cutright, P. 1974. "The Civilian Earnings of White and Black Draftees and Nonveterans." *American Sociological Review* 39 (no. 3):317–327.

DeTray, D. 1982. "Veterans Status as a Screening Device." *American Economic Review* 72 (no. 1):133–142.

Fredland, J., and R. Little. 1980. "Long-Term Returns to Vocational Training: Evidence from Military Sources." *Journal of Human Resources* 15 (no. 1):49–66.

Griliches, Z. 1976. "Wages of Very Young Men." *Journal of Political Economy 84,* (no. 4, pt. 2):569–585.

———— and W. Mason. 1972. "Education, Income and Ability." *Journal of Political Economy 80* (no. 3, pt. 2):S74–S103.

Heckman, J. 1976. "The Common Structure of Statistical Models of Truncation, Sample Selection and Limited Dependent Variables and a Simple Estimator for Such Models." *Annals of Economic and Social Measurement:* 475–492.

———— and S. Polachek. 1974. "Empirical Evidence on the Functional Form of the Earnings-Schooling Relationship." *Journal of the American Statistical Association 69:* 350–354.

Houthakker, H. 1959. "Education and Income." *Review of Economics and Statistics 41:* 24–28.

Kassing, D. 1970. "Military Experience as a Determinant of Veteran's Earnings." *Studies Prepared for President's Commission on All-Volunteer Armed Forces,* Vol. 2. Washington, D.C.: U.S. Government Printing Office.

Kim, C., and J. Jackson. 1983. "Wage Growth Rates of Young Men: A Longitudinal Analysis." Columbus, Ohio: Center for Human Resource Research.

King, A., and C. Knapp. 1978. "Race and the Determinants of Lifetime Earnings." *Industrial and Labor Relations Review 31* (no. 3):347–355.

Kohen, A., et al. 1977. *Career Thresholds: Longitudinal Studies of the Education and Labor Market Experiences of Young Men,* Vol. 6. Columbus, Ohio: Center for Human Resource Research.

Mincer, J. 1958. "Investments in Human Capital and Personal Income Distribution." *Journal of Political Economy 66* (no. 4):281–302.

————. 1974. *Schooling, Experience and Earnings.* New York: National Bureau for Economic Research.

National Advisory Commission on Selective Service. 1967. *In Pursuit of Equity: Who Serves When Not All Serve?* Washington, D.C.: U.S. Government Printing Office.

Norrblum, E. 1976. *The Returns to Military and Civilian Training.* Santa Monica, Calif.: Rand Corporation.

Oi, W. 1967. "The Economic Cost of the Draft." *American Economic Review 57* (no. 2):39–63.

Stiglitz, J. 1975. "The Theory of Screening, Education and the Distribution of Income." *American Economic Review 65* (no. 3):283–300.

Veterans Administration. 1981. *Data on Vietnam Era Veterans.* Washington, D.C.: Office of Reports and Statistics.

Wolpin, K. 1977. "Education and Screening." *American Economic Review 67* (no. 5): 949–958.

8
Skill Transfer and Military Occupational Training

Stephen Mangum
David Ball

T he end of the Vietnam War and the advent of voluntary service in the
armed forces fundamentally altered the relationship that prevailed
for decades between the military and civilian sectors of our economy.
With the formal ending of hostilities and the demise of the draft, greater
choice was available to the nation's youth regarding military service. The
decision as to whether to enter the military became a less constrained choice
after the Vietnam War. This chapter focuses on data from the postwar period
to investigate a single issue, skill transfer between military service and civilian
employment.

Why might a young man freely choose to enlist in the military? More
than 30 percent of males in the Youth Cohort of the National Longitudinal
Surveys (NLS) of Labor Force Experience who enlisted in the armed forces by
1979 said "training opportunities" were their prime motivation for enlistment. Another 15 percent listed "money for a college education" as the major
reason, and 17 percent entered the military to "better myself in life." In contrast, 9 percent said "travel" was their prime motivation, while 8 percent of
the young men entered the military to "serve my country." One percent of the
enlistees responding expected to receive higher wages in the military than in
the civilian economy (Kim, 1982).[1]

These figures suggest that many young men see the military as (1) providing skill development that "pays off" in net benefits over their entire working
life, or (2) providing benefits that permit further investment in human capital
that eventually yield positive net benefits, or both. That they choose the military suggests they see this institution as helping them reach their goals (educational or other) more efficiently than would be possible through other means.
Indeed, the military is the single largest vocational training institution in the
country. For fiscal year 1983 the Department of Defense requested a training
budget of $12.8 billion to support a training load of 254,726 individuals
(full-time equivalents).[2]

In view of the predominance of a desire for education and training (either via occupational skill training and in-service education provided by the military or access to postservice educational benefit programs that a successful tour of duty affords) as the stated motivation for enlistment, it is surprising how few individuals in the NLS sample report that they use skills acquired in the military in civilian employment. Only 12.4 percent of male veterans and 5.0 percent of male attriters in a representative group of NLS respondents reported any use in their later civilian jobs of occupational skills acquired in the military. This apparent inconsistency is particularly striking in that 80 percent of military occupational specialties have counterparts in the civilian sector (McFann, 1976; Weinstein, 1967).

What is the wisdom of a human capital investment strategy that involves the military? One factor among the several likely to influence the market valuation of military experience is whether or not individuals are able to transfer their military training to civilian employment. Previous studies looking at whether skills acquired in the military are used in the civilian sector and whether use of this training influences postmilitary labor market outcomes have generally found rather low utilization of military-acquired skills in the civilian sector, and little, if any, increase in earnings due to the use of skills acquired through training provided by the military.[3] The finding of low reported utilization of military-acquired skills is consistent with the evidence from the NLS reported here. The finding of no earnings impact appears at odds with the oftstated motivation for enlistment—the investment motivation. Why the apparent inconsistency? If expectations prompting enlistment are not realized, why doesn't that information alter behavior among those considering enlistment?

Our sample for exploring the transferability of training acquired in the military includes young men from the NLS youth cohort who, at the initial interview date in 1979, reported being last currently enrolled in school after July 1, 1975 but prior to December 31, 1978, and who chose to enter the military at some point during the 1975 to 1978 period. As of the 1983 interview date, of the 705 young men meeting these restrictions, 48.2 percent (340) had completed an enlistment and left the military, 139 (19.7 percent) had left the military prior to completing a full enlistment, and 226 (32.1 percent) had completed a tour of duty and were still serving in the military. Our interest here is on the 479 individuals who served in the military and returned to the civilian world by 1983.

The Extent of Skill Transfer

Concern with the small amount of skill transfer suggested by the respondents' self-reporting—12.4 percent for veterans, 5 percent for those who left the military without completing a full enlistment (hereafter referred to as non-completers or "attriters")—led us to analyze individual work histories.

Occupational specialties while in the armed forces were compared to the occupations held by each veteran and non-completer during their period of postmilitary civilian employment. In excess of 80 percent had held military occupational specialties having civilian counterparts (that is, they were in noncombat arms specialties). In comparing military and postmilitary occupations, a "match" was determined to occur when the military occupation and the postmilitary civilian occupation were virtually identical: a tank mechanic in the military and a heavy equipment mechanic in civilian life, or military police in the armed forces and police/detective in the civilian world, for example. A broader category of "probable match" was defined to include all cases of "match" and cases where the skill overlap between military and civilian occupation was highly probable; for example, administrative specialty in the armed forces and office manager in civilian employment or food services specialist in the military and restaurant manager in the civilian world.[4]

Military training-civilian employment matches were identified in 22.5 percent of the cases for veterans in which valid information was available[5] and in 21.8 percent of the noncompleter cases. A probable occupational match was found in 35 percent of both the veteran and noncompleter cases. Throughout the remainder of this chapter all references to occupational match mean the more restrictive of the two definitions.

These numbers suggest much greater skill transfer between the military and civilian sectors than evidenced by the self-reporting of the survey respondents. The results from the analysis of work histories are consequently more consistent with expectations based on the stated motivations for enlistment than are the results from respondent self-reporting. While many factors might account for this difference, it is likely that individuals, in responding to the survey question, do not dissect their military and civilian occupations into individual skills and analyze overlaps on that basis. The tendency is probably to make comparison at the level of occupational titles rather than at the level of skills and duties.

Table 8–1 reports the distribution of occupational matches by sex, race, educational attainment, Armed Forces Qualifications Test (AFQT) score, branch of military service, length of time in the military, and military occupational specialty. A greater percentage of whites than minorities in the sample were able to transfer occupational skills acquired in the military to civilian employment. Individuals having served in the navy or the air force experienced a significantly greater percentage occupational match, 42.5 and 43.3 percent respectively, than did those who served in the army or marines (29.8 percent). Those serving on active duty for less than 2 years before returning to the civilian sector were more likely to find a civilian job making use of skills acquired in the military than were those serving more than 2 years but

Table 8–1
Percentage of Cases Exhibiting Military-Civilian Occupational Match, by Selected Characteristics

		N
Race		
Minority	26.1	87
White	37.3	327
Education		
Some high school	31.2	88
High school graduate	37.2	300
Some college	27.9	26
Branch of service		
Army/marines[b]	29.8	245
Air force	43.3	66
Navy	42.5	103
AFQT[c]		
Highest quintile	28.5	137
Fourth quintile	45.9	149
Middle quintile	23.6	79
Second quintile	30.5	10
Active duty		
Up to 2 years	38.2	37
2 to 4 years	29.0	182
More than 4 years	40.0	195
Military occupation		
Combat arms[d]	10.1	115
Electronic equipment repair	14.4	25
Communications/intelligence	19.6	26
Medical care	50.6	13
Administration	37.4	42
Electrical/mechanical equipment repair	56.2	119
Craftsman	51.9	18
Service/support	41.4	56

Note: For sample described in the text, percentages based on weighted values.

[b]These two services branches were combined in this and in subsequent tables because the number of marines in the data set was insufficient to permit separate analysis.

[c]No one in the sample of those having served in the military had an AFQT score in the lowest quintile.

[d]Includes classification "not elsewhere occupationally qualified."

less than 4 years. The percentage with an occupational match increased for those serving 4 years or more. The latter fact may reflect differences in completion status, since the typical enlistment period is 4 years in length. Finally, table 8–1 suggests particularly sizable levels of skill transfer among those who served in medical care, electrical and mechanical equipment repair, crafts, and service occupations while in the military.

Improvements in educational attainment are also consistent with the motivations for enlistment reviewed earlier. In our sample of individuals, 31.8 percent of those who served in the military and returned to the civilian world by 1983 increased their educational attainment by at least 1 year over the 1979 to 1983 period. Combining these figures on educational attainment with those on military-civilian skill transfer, we find that 53.8 percent of the veterans and 51.1 percent of the noncompleters in the sample experienced outcomes consistent with their stated motivations for enlistment.[6] These percentages are much more consistent with a priori expectations than are the results of respondents' self-reporting as to whether or not they made use, in civilian employment, of skills acquired in the military. The analysis of work histories lends support to the notion of military service as part of a rational human capital investment strategy.

Some Correlates of Skill Transferability

Table 8–2 presents logistic estimates of the effect of various factors on the probability that an individual will locate civilian employment in an occupation related to his military occupation. Included in this analysis are all veterans and attriters in the sample for whom sufficient information exists to determine whether or not an occupational match occurred. The dependent variable has a value of 1 if the respondent's work history indicates a match between military occupation and occupation of postmilitary employment; and 0 otherwise. The independent variables included in table 8–2 are self-explanatory.

The sole significant determinant of the probability of finding an occupational match between military and civilian sectors that emerges from this analysis is the type of occupational training received while in the military. Individuals trained in medical care, administration, electrical or mechanical equipment repair, or the service occupations while in the military were significantly more likely to find employment in a related civilian occupation than were those receiving training in the combat arms occupations while in the military. Controlling for type of military training, there was no significant difference in the probability of an occupational match by race, by branch of

Table 8–2
Logistic Estimates of the Effect of Military Occupational Specialty and Other Variables on the Probability of a Military-Civilian Occupational Match

	Coefficient	Standard Error
Independent variables		
AFQT score	.002	(.011)[a]
Highest grade completed	−.035	(.171)
Minority	−.212	(.381)
Branch of service[a]		
Air Force	.201	(.391)
Navy	.175	(.362)
Active duty (weeks)	.0007	(.003)
Completion status[b]		
Veteran	−.557	(.412)
Military occupation[c]		
Electronic equipment repair	−.546	(1.113)
Communications/intelligence	−.914	(1.101)
Medical care	2.071***	(.741)
Administration	1.780***	(.547)
Electrical/mechanical equipment repair	1.862***	(.463)
Craftsman	1.200	(.793)
Service/support	2.319***	(.505)
Intercept	−2.036	(1.919)
-2 log likelihood	345.10	
Chi square	53.84	
Sample size	375	

[a]"Army/marines" omitted.
[b]"Combat arms" and "not otherwise classified" omitted.
***Significant at .01 level.

service, or by length of time spent on active duty. Similarly, there is no evidence here of a credentialing or screening effect relative to veteran státus (DeTray, 1982; Berger and Hirsch, 1983). Controlling for military occupation and length of time on active duty, a proxy for the experience component of military service, veterans were no more likely to achieve a military-civilian occupational match than were those individuals who left the military prior to completing a full enlistment.

The Impact of Skill Transfer on
Labor Market Outcomes

Some suggestion of the possible impact of skill transfer upon labor market outcomes is given by the following figures. The mean 1983 hourly rate of pay for veterans in our sample who located an occupational match at some point in their postmilitary employment history was $6.23, in comparison to $5.79 for those veterans not finding a match. For noncompleters the difference in mean hourly rates of pay was even larger, with a mean of $6.71 for those having found an occupational match and $4.82 for those who had not.[7] These simple means suggest that finding civilian employment that makes use of training acquired in the military does contribute, on average, to postmilitary labor market success. Yet these differences might be wholly or partially attributable to a number of other factors.

Human capital theory posits that the acquisition of knowledge and skills through schooling, training, and work experience yields improvement in individual earnings and other labor market outcomes, such as employment stability, through the mechanism of increased productivity. Among individuals who have served in the armed forces, completion status, length of postmilitary work experience, and the transferability of skill training acquired in the military would appear important in any assessment of the impact of military service on labor market outcomes. To analyze these effects and identify key relationships, we turn to a multivariate analysis of factors determining labor market outcomes among our sample of veterans and individuals who left the military prior to completing a full enlistment.

A number of variables are introduced to proxy the theoretical constructs of schooling, training, work experience, and individual and job characteristics mentioned earlier. Educational attainment is represented by the respondent's *Highest Grade Completed*. *AFQT Score* is included as a measure of ability or achievement.[8] The influence of race is proxied by a variable that has the value of 1 if the respondent is a minority (black or Hispanic), 0 otherwise. The variable *Married* differentiates between respondents who are married and living with their spouses and those living under any other arrangement (for example, single or divorced). *Health* proxies whether or not the individual has any health problems limiting work alternatives.

From a human capital perspective it is anticipated that the better educated and more achievement oriented in the sample should have greater labor market success. It is thought that being married exercises a stabilizing influence in the lives of young men which should be linked to labor market success. Because of a myriad of factors, including differential access to training opportunities, differences in average socioeconomic background, and the continued existence of racial discrimination of many types, it is hypothesized that racial minorities will, on average, experience more difficult times in labor market activity than will the racial majority.

The possible influence of geographic factors is represented by two variables: *South Residence* distinguishes between respondents residing in the South as opposed to some other region of the United States; and *SMSA Residence* differentiates those living in a Standard Metropolitan Statistical Area from those residing elsewhere. SMSAs are thought to offer greater employment options than other areas. Wage rates have historically been lower in the South, though some recent evidence suggests that this is changing. Another variable, *Collective Bargaining,* is included to proxy the influence of collective bargaining agreements on labor market outcomes. It is hypothesized that coverage by collective bargaining will be related to labor market success.

A couple of variables enter the analysis as controls for differences in work experience across respondents. The length of time the respondent has been employed by his current or last employer (*Tenure*) is included as a measure of firm-specific skill acquisition and seniority rights. An attempt is made to account for differences in civilian versus military work experience under the expectation that civilian employers might view some military time as institution-specific and therefore not as valuable in the civilian labor market as civilian work experience. To explore this hypothesis, the variable, *Civilian Employment,* records the number of weeks of civilian employment for each respondent from January 1, 1978 to the date of the 1983 interview.[9] A separate variable, *Military Work Experience,* measures weeks on active duty over the same time period.

A number of additional constructs are employed to look at questions about military service and labor market outcomes. The variable *Veteran* differentiates between individuals who completed at least one full enlistment and those who left the military prior to completing an enlistment. The question of whether locating a civilian occupation that makes use of skills acquired in the military influences labor market outcomes is explored by the variable *Match,* which takes a value of 1 where the individual was determined to have found such an occupational skill match. The a priori expectation is that achieving a military-civilian skill match should have a positive influence on the labor market success of those in the sample. Whether the type of occupational training provided by the military exercises any influence on labor market outcomes, independent of whether or not a match exists between military and civilian occupations, is investigated by including a series of occupation dummies in the analysis. Possible interaction between occupational category and occupational match is investigated with a second set of dummies.

Three different measures of labor market outcomes served as dependent variables: hourly rate of pay at time of 1983 interview, weeks unemployed since the last interview as reported in 1983, and 1983 wage and salary income. The results reported here are limited to the hourly rate of pay regressions.[10]

Results

Results of the hourly wage equation are presented in table 8–3. *AFQT Score, SMSA Residence,* and having wages set by collective bargaining had consistently positive impacts on hourly rate of pay. Hourly pay increased significantly with additional weeks of tenure (firm-specific experience) and with additional weeks of general work experience. Veterans in the sample recorded significantly higher hourly wage rates than did noncompleters after controlling for other factors. Finding civilian employment that made use of occupational skills acquired in the military significantly increased the individual's hourly rate of pay above that of individuals not experiencing a match of military and civilian occupational skills. These results are consistent with a priori expectations.

Column 2 of table 8–3 includes occupational area of military skill training in the hourly rate of pay equation, while column 3 permits interaction between occupational area of military training and whether or not a military-civilian occupational match occurred. The results suggest that, after controlling for other factors, the occupational area of military training does not contribute to explaining variations in hourly pay rates across individuals. In both cases, comparing either specification 2 or 3 to specification 1, the tabulated value of *F* exceeds that calculated for the equation.[11] In specification 2, individuals receiving occupational training in the administrative and service occupations while in the military averaged significantly less in hourly pay in 1983 than did those trained in the combat arms classifications, after controlling for other factors. In specification 3, with the addition of the interaction term, the coefficient on the occupational match variable is no longer significant.

Conclusions

This chapter documents greater transfer of occupational skills between the military and civilian sectors than has been characteristic of earlier research of this kind. The data set differs from those of most previous studies in that it includes individuals who both entered and exited from the military since the demise of the draft. The possibility of increased choice of military occupational specialty under this regime may contribute to the finding of more skill transfer. Similarly, with the increased technological sophistication of today's military and the reduced importance of combat arms positions, military work today more closely resembles civilian jobs than was true in the past. These

Table 8–3
Regression of (Ln) Hourly Wage on Selected Characteristics of 1975–78 NLS Cohort of Males: 1983

	Specification 1		Specification 2		Specification 3	
	Coefficient	t-ratio	Coefficient	t-ratio	Coefficient	t-ratio
Independent variables						
Highest grade completed	−0.011	(−.41)	−0.005	(−.19)	−0.007	(−.24)
AFQT score	0.005***	(3.04)	0.005***	(2.86)	0.005***	(2.86)
South residence	0.069	(1.40)	0.073	(1.46)	0.066	(1.30)
SMSA residence	0.140**	(2.53)	0.135**	(2.41)	0.130**	(2.27)
Married	0.075	(1.51)	0.076	(1.50)	0.068	(1.30)
Veteran	0.178***	(2.73)	0.204***	(3.08)	0.208***	(3.07)
Minority	−0.021	(−.35)	−0.022	(−.36)	−0.019	(−.30)
Collective bargaining	0.303***	(5.29)	0.293***	(5.09)	0.290***	(4.91)
Health	−0.083	(−.30)	−0.117	(−.42)	−0.136	(−.48)
Match	0.122**	(2.14)	0.184***	(2.96)	−0.142	(−.70)
Tenure	0.002***	(3.51)	0.002***	(3.34)	0.002***	(3.29)
Civilian employment	0.002***	(2.84)	0.002***	(2.82)	0.002***	(2.60)
Military work experience	0.00001	(.01)	−0.00006	(−.09)	−0.00001	(−.23)
Military occupation						
Electronic equipment repair			0.062	(.58)	0.035	(.32)

Skill Transfer and Military Occupational Training • 143

	(1)	(2)	(3)
Communications/intelligence		0.029 (.32)	−0.001 (.02)
Medical care		−0.160 (−1.20)	−0.290 (−1.59)
Administration		−0.169* (−1.83)	−0.205* (−1.92)
Electrical/mechanical equipment repair		−0.067 (−1.00)	−0.070 (−.95)
Craftsman		0.040 (.31)	0.015 (.10)
Service/support		−0.149* (−1.78)	−0.180* (−1.78)
Military occupation times match			
Electronic equipment repair			0.513 (1.14)
Communication/intelligence			0.662 (1.48)
Medical care			0.558* (1.74)
Administration			0.395 (1.51)
Electrical/mechanical equipment repair			0.292 (1.29)
Craftsman			0.390 (1.04)
Service/support			0.364 (1.49)
Intercept	5.340*** (16.71)	5.324*** (16.40)	5.381*** (16.20)
Adjusted R^2	.26	.26	.25
Sample size	292	292	292

Note: Cohort restrictions as explained in text.
*Significant at .10 level.
**Significant at .05 level.
***Significant at .01 level.

points are particularly important as the reader compares the analysis in this chapter with that of the preceding chapter. Chapter 7 looks at the effects of military service during wartime (the Vietnam War). The combination of the draft and wartime conditions limited the amount of choice the system offered relative to military training. Further, the demands of war increased the number of young men in combat arms occupations, offering the lowest probability of skill transfer to the civilian sector. Thus the finding in chapter 7 that the labor market places little value on training received in the military must be taken in historical context.

A large percentage of those in the sample cite a desire for education and training as their motivation for enlistment. The evidence suggests that the majority of these individuals do in fact achieve their education and training goals through the military. An effort to compare military and civilian occupations offers evidence of greater skill transfer than visible in respondent self-reporting. It is likely that a detailed task analysis of military and civilian employments would yield even greater transferability than suggested here.

In this study, occupational type of military training is found to be a key variable explaining differences in the probability of a military-civilian occupational match across individuals in the sample. Individuals locating civilian employment for which their military training is relevant do significantly better in terms of hourly rate of pay than do those not locating a military-civilian skill match. These findings are consistent with the statements of young enlistees that they enter the miltary for the education and training opportunities provided by the military. It must be stressed that while presenting evidence that skills acquired in the military and transferred to the civilian sector pay off in higher wages after controlling for work experience, education, and so forth, this chapter says *nothing* about the labor market status of individuals choosing to serve in the military relative to individuals of similar characteristics who choose not to serve.

Controlling for whether or not the individual had transferred his military-acquired occupational skills to the civilian sector, inclusion of the occupational area of the military training did not significantly increase the explanatory power of the wage equation investigated. These findings suggest that the postmilitary value of alternative types of military occupational training depends largely upon whether the training is subsequently used in the civilian sector. Based on this sample, the military occupation an individual is trained in is of little economic importance if he does not enter civilian employment that makes use of the skills acquired in the military. The evidence suggests that some military occupations do offer better military-civilian occupational linkages than others. The transferability of training acquired in the military to civilian employment is a key determinant of the economic value of the training.

Notes

1. Several studies in the sociology literature view patriotism to be a more important motivation for enlistment than suggested by these raw percentages. Burk (1984) is a representative piece from this literature and uses NLS data in making its argument.

2. Department of Defense, *Military Manpower Training Report for FY1983,* March 1982, p. 9. This amount includes pay and allowances for trainees and training support personnel, training operations, and training-related procurement, but does not include costs associated with on-the-job training.

3. Among the studies that have investigated these issues are those of Giesecke (1973), Jurkowitz (1969), Massell and Nelson (1974), O'Neill, Ross, and Warner (1978), Richardson (1968), Weinstein (1969), Winkler and Thompson (1971), Biderman (1976), and Fredland and Little (1980). Winkler and Thompson (1971) and Richardson (1968) are exceptions to the rule concerning low utilization of military training. Giesecke (1973), Norrblom (1976), and O'Neill et al. (1978) found evidence that use in civilian employment of skills learned in the military influences earnings. Fredland and Little (1980) found long-term impacts to military training.

4. Determination of military-civilian skill or occupation transfer was made by comparing an individual's military occupational code to the Bureau of Census Standard Occupation Classification (SOC) code of any postmilitary jobs held. This exercise was completed prior to the availability of and completely independent of the Defense Department's Military-Civilian Occupational Crosscode Project.

5. To be considered a valid case, the individual had to have reported a military occupation and at least one postmilitary occupational code. Sufficient information existed to determine whether or not a match had occurred in 93.2 percent of the veteran cases and 69.8 percent of the attriter cases.

6. These percentages control for the fact that some individuals had an increase in educational attainment *and* a military-civilian occupational match. These percentages may underestimate additional skill acquisition in that they do not account for individuals participating in programs offered by business and technical institutes, area vocational schools, companies, proprietary schools, and other schools.

7. To be included in this and subsequent analyses individuals in the sample had to have reported wage and salary income or an hourly rate of pay in 1983.

8. There is a sizable literature which uses AFQT score as a measure of inherent ability, while another literature refers to it exclusively as a measure of knowledge or achievement. An extensive study of the Armed Forces Vocational Aptitude Battery from which the AFQT is drawn is found in Profiles of American Youth, Office of the Assistant Secretary of Defense, 1982.

9. For most respondents this variable records the number of weeks employed between the date they left the military and the 1983 interview date. However, week-by-week civilian employment data is unavailable in the data set for individuals in the sample entering and leaving the military prior to January 1, 1978. Their civilian employment experience is counted beginning with January 1, 1978.

10. Tables summarizing results from the other regressions are available from the authors upon request.

11. Comparing specifications 1 and 2, the calculated F is 1.24. Critical values for $F_{7,272}$ are 4.61 at the 1 percent level and 3.00 at the 5 percent level. For specification 3

relative to 1, the calculated F is .96, while the critical values for $F_{14,272}$ are 2.04 and 1.67 for the 1 and 5 percent levels, respectively.

References

Berger, Mark C., and Barry T. Hirsch. 1983. "The Civilian Earnings Experience of Viet Nam Era Veterans." *Journal of Human Resources 18* (no. 4, Fall).

Biderman, A.D. 1976. "Relationships between Active Duty and Post-Retirement Careers." In N. Wilson, ed., *Manpower Research*. London: English Universities Press.

Burk, James. 1984. "Patriotism and the All-Volunteer Force." *Journal of Political and Military Sociology 12* (Fall).

DeTray, Dennis. 1982. "Veteran Status as a Screening Device." *American Economic Review 72* (no. 1, March).

Fredland, J., and R. Little. 1980. "Long Term Returns to Vocational Training: Evidence from Military Sources." *Journal of Human Resources 15* (no. 1, March).

Giesecke, L. 1973. "The Relationship between Military and Civilian Occupations and Early Post-Service Earnings: Army Enlisted Personnel Separating 7/68 through 9/69." Defense Manpower Data Center Staff Paper.

Jurkowitz, E. 1969. "An Estimation of the Military Contribution to Human Capital." Appendix E of *The Final Report of the Military Training Study*, Department of Economics, University of Maryland, College Park, Md.

Kim, C. 1982. "Youth and the Military Services: 1980 National Longitudinal Survey Studies of Enlistment, Intentions to Serve, Reenlistment and Labor Market Experience of Veterans and Attriters." Columbus, Ohio: Center for Human Resource Research, May.

Massell, A., and G. Nelson. 1974. *The Estimation of Training Premiums for U.S. Military Personnel*. P5250, Santa Monica, Calif.: Rand Corporation, June.

McFann, H. 1976. "Training for the Military." Human Resource Research Organization, Alexandria, Va.

Nestel, G. 1983. "Military Service and Civilian Wages: Another Look." Columbus, Ohio: Center for Human Resource Research, July.

Norrblom, E. 1976. *The Returns to Military and Civilian Training*. R-1900-ARPR. Santa Monica, Calif.: Rand Corporation.

O'Neill, D., S. Ross, and J. Warner. 1978. "Military Occupation, G.I. Bill Training, and Human Capital." In R.V.L. Cooper, ed., *Defense Manpower Policy*. Santa Monica, Calif.: Rand Corporation.

Richardson, R.B. 1968. *Transferring Military Experience to Civilian Jobs*. Manpower/Automation Research Monograph No. 8. Washington, D.C.: Manpower Administration, U.S. Department of Labor, Oct.

U.S. Department of Commerce, Bureau of Census. 1982. *Alphabetical Index of Industries and Occupations: The 1980 Census of Population*. Washington, D.C.: U.S. Government Printing Office.

U.S. Department of Defense. 1982. *Occupational Conversion Manual, Enlisted/Officer/Civilian*. Washington, D.C.

Weinstein, P. 1967. "Occupational Crossover and Universal Military Training." In Sol Tax, ed., *The Draft: A Handbook of Facts and Alternatives.* Chicago: University of Chicago Press.

———. 1969. *Final Report of the Military Training Study.* College Park: University of Maryland, Department of Economics.

Winkler, A., and P. Thompson. 1971. "Post Service Utilization of Air Force-Gained Skills." Alexandria, Va.: Air Force Human Resources Laboratory, Manpower Development Division, Sept.

9
How Fluid Is the U.S. Labor Market?

Stephen M. Hills

L abor markets work well when workers are allocated efficiently to jobs where their skills are well utilized, when adequate information is provided for individuals to make reasonable choices about future employment, and when such information is provided without reference to personal characteristics such as race and sex.

Whether labor markets fulfill these functions might be evaluated through aggregate measures of unemployment, but in a free society, some degree of unemployment must occur even in the most effective labor market systems. Whether or not unemployment exceeds its necessary minimum amount is a matter of opinion and often of heated debate.

Because unemployment is hard to interpret, in this book other measures of how U.S. labor markets function have been used. The indicators were the degree of interindustry mobility across the business cycle, geographic mobility, earnings losses due to involuntary job separations, the amount by which government transfer payments and the earnings of other family members reduce the unemployment costs of changing jobs, the appearance of distinct career patterns in the working lives of young men, the effect of military service on subsequent earnings, the transferability of skills from military to civilian jobs, and the degree to which these indicators differed by race once other factors such as education and work experience were held constant.

Use of these indicators does not avoid the problem of determining an optimal amount for each, because value judgments are still necessary to assess what is high or low. Where possible, other time periods were used as were other sources of data or other definitions of the problem, but in the end, the reader must determine whether the indicators are high or low.

The indicators and the modeling of individual behavior yield evidence about how labor markets work, but predictions about how they *should* work have been a matter of controversy. Theory based on the presumption of perfect competition predicts that labor markets will be fluid, with individual workers seeking out their best alternatives by shifting readily from firm to firm or from region to region. External shocks to the system (such as a dramatic change in technology or a sudden increase in the price of raw materials) will be accommodated by changes in the relative prices of products and relative wage rates. Workers will then change where they work or live based on changes in wage rates.

A different theoretical tradition places emphasis on structural barriers to adjustment in the labor market and downplays both the fluidity of markets and worker adaptation to change. An early proponent of this view referred to labor markets as "balkanized" (Kerr, 1954), and theorists since then have identified a number of factors which divide labor markets into isolated "nation states." Regionalism and the establishment of strong ties with families and friends restrict geographic mobility. Internal labor markets develop within firms, both as a response to the costs of high turnover and to the threat of unionization, causing industrial mobility to fall (Jacoby, 1983). Discrimination in hiring practices, combined with internal labor markets, create dual or segmented markets where workers who are assigned the worst jobs in the economy find it difficult to move into better employment (Gorden, 1972; Hodson, 1984). Throughout this book, the data detail the situations in which one or the other view of the labor market is more appropriate, but, not surprisingly, neither view is true in the extreme.

Interindustry and geographic mobility provide a good picture of the volume of activity accommodated by U.S. labor markets and are straightforward measures of the fluidity of the market. In this book, the jobs that young men held in the late 1970s were divided into 25 industrial classifications (for example, motor vehicles, primary metals, textiles, business and repair services), and a substantial amount of interindustry mobility across the 1973–78 business cycle was found. The results from chapter 3 show that almost half of the young men whose labor market data were analyzed left the industry in which they were employed in 1973 and had not returned again by 1978. These men were not teenagers exploring the market for their first full-time jobs: they were age 26–36 in 1978, most of them old enough to have completed both high school and college.

The degree of mobility isolated implies that many young men first employed in industries with declining employment opportunities can and do switch to industries with better prospects. The average mobility rate out of the motor vehicles and metals industries was 52 percent; from all other durable goods industries, 58 percent; and from industries in the service sector (professional services, banking, and public utilities, for example), only 45 percent.

NLS data measure the degree of adjustment for young workers; 1970 Census data yield good comparisons of adjustment across industries for men of all ages. Census data on interindustry mobility rates show that 28 percent of men age 25–34 who were employed in 1965 were, by 1970, employed in a different one of the 10 industry grouping used by Census to classify jobs.

Since the Census data are based on much broader classifications than ours, they are not directly comparable, but they show what happens as young men age. At age 35–49, only 17 percent of men had changed industries, and at age 50–64 only 13 percent (U.S. Department of the Commerce, 1973, pp. 62–63).

A significant number of young men also changed geographic location during the 1970s. Chapter 5 showed that over a 5-year period (1976–81), 30 percent of young men moved from one city or town to another (if they lived in rural areas, moves were from one county to another). The figures on mobility are slightly higher than those calculated by the U.S. Department of Labor's *Current Population Survey,* but CPS figures are from county to county in all cases. CPS data show that in 1980, 26 percent of men age 29–39 had moved from one county to another in the previous 5-year period (U.S. Department of Commerce, 1981).

Figures on geographic mobility alone cannot establish how well labor markets work because many moves are made for reasons unrelated to employment. Chapter 5 linked NLS data on geographic mobility with data on job changes and found that between 1976 and 1981 only 16 percent of NLS young men moved their residences and also changed where they worked. Furthermore, about 30 percent of those who moved and changed work sites stated that neither their own employment nor the employment of their wives was a reason for the move. Thus labor markets had an effective influence on decisions about geographic location for just over 10 percent of this youthful sample of young men. Compared with their industrial mobility, young men's geographic mobility in response to changing employment requirements was relatively modest.

CPS data show that men in the NLS survey (men age 29–39 in 1981) are among the most mobile of any age. As of 1980, CPS mobility rates started at 16 percent for men age 18, peaked at 37 percent for men age 26, and fell steadily again to 17 percent for men age 39. If employment-related reasons are linked with the geographic mobility decisions of so few young men, the number of older men who move for work-related reasons must be negligible indeed.

The third indicator of labor market adjustment was the change in hourly earnings associated with involuntary job loss. Excluding the construction industry, where involuntary job shifts are often associated with seasonality, we found that displaced workers earned on average 9 percent less than they might have expected to earn had they not lost their jobs (chapter 2). This average earnings loss was measured a little more than 2 years following displacement. For a second sample of displaced workers (containing many, though not all, of the workers in the first sample), it was found that the average hourly wage 9 months after displacement was again 9 percent less than the wage we expected for nondisplaced workers.

Is the aforementioned degree of wage loss high or low? For the NLS sample of young workers, we might expect little or no wage loss, assuming that shifts in careers and geographic locations are easier for younger than older workers. Indeed, an earlier longitudinal study of older workers measured a much larger fall in hourly earnings due to displacement than did chapter 2—a 38 percent drop in 1976 earnings for those displaced between 1971 and 1975 (Parnes et al., 1979, p. 82). The method of analysis differs significantly between the earlier study and the present one, and consequently the two estimates of wage loss can be only roughly compared. Nevertheless, the estimated degree of loss for workers who were age 50–59 in 1971 places into context the measures we have obtained.

Offsetting the losses in earnings which occur due to involuntary job loss are government transfer payments, most notably unemployment insurance. Also helping to cushion the costs of unemployment are the earnings of other family members. In chapter 5, the author asked which of these two factors was most important by measuring the effect of each on the number of weeks of unemployment that a young man experienced in 1981. She assumed that young men, to some extent, decide how long they will be unemployed (a standard assumption of job search theory), and asked which factor had the strongest influence on the decision to be unemployed. Whichever factor was strongest was then presumed to be more important in offsetting the costs of unemployment.

A 33 percent increase in weekly unemployment income raised the proportion of time spent unemployed by about 5 percent and a comparable 33 percent increase in wife's annual income raised the proportion of time spent unemployed by 3 percent. When measured by its impact on behavior, unemployment income was, therefore, a more important offset for the costs of unemployment than was wife's income, but neither factor was very important in lengthening the duration of unemployment.

A good way of measuring the adaptability of labor markets is to observe an outside event which would disrupt the market's allocational mechanism or, at the very least, put strain on the market's ability to place people in new jobs. One such event was the Vietnam War, whose effects were examined in chapter 7. If military service had disrupted careers sufficiently, a negative relationship would have been shown between military service and a worker's subsequent earnings or stability of employment. Instead, chapter 7 found that service during the Vietnam War raised subsequent earnings for whites and left the earnings of blacks unaffected. The experience obtained during military service was not what was rewarded in subsequent civilian employment, but rather employers appear to have discriminated in favor of veterans by paying a premium for the military "credential." The effects of military service on earnings do not, therefore, signal a market failure to reemploy veterans in jobs comparable to the ones that nonveterans would have had. On the other hand, military service was weakly associated with decreased employment stability among blacks, and whites with high ability received a lower wage premium after serving than did whites with low ability.

The fact that military service affects subsequent earnings through the credentials conferred on individuals implies that labor markets place little value on the training men receive in the military, despite claims to the contrary for the all-voluntary armed forces. In chapter 8 the mechanism for skill transfer from military to civilian jobs was analyzed using a sample of data from the post-Vietnam era. The authors asked whether skills which matched well between the military and civilian sectors were rewarded more.

The initial data implied that skills were not being transferred from military to civilian jobs at a very high rate: even though 80 percent of military occupational specialties have civilian counterparts, only 12 percent of male veterans reported that their civilian jobs made use of skills acquired in the military. Self-reports for the usefulness of skills acquired in other jobs or in formal training may not be reliable if individuals define the skills they have acquired quite narrowly. Indeed, when military and civilian jobs were matched using standard occupational codings, the authors of chapter 8 found that 23 percent of the military and civilian jobs matched exactly and in another 13 percent of the cases, the match between occupations was quite close. Furthermore, for the sample of men who served in the post-Vietnam era, the match between military and civilian occupations paid off, a match resulting in a 20 percent increase in hourly wages, all else constant. These results indicate that for about a third of male veterans from the post-Vietnam era, military experience should have a positive effect on subsequent earnings, an effect which is the result of a match of occupational skills and not solely credentialing.

Although chapter 8 gives a different view of the functioning of the labor market than chapter 7, the results can be reconciled. Military objectives and the motivations of young men to enter military service were very different in the two time periods studied. During the Vietnam War, the objective for many military units was combat, not training. After the war, however, the armed forces placed increased emphasis on training as a means of recruiting volunteers. Employers in the post-Vietnam period may hire veterans based on the skills they have acquired, whereas Vietnam veterans may have been hired because of their military service, not because of their skills. On the other hand, the differences between chapters 7 and 8 may be due simply to different methods of statistical analysis. In chapter 7, only the total length of time in military service was measured and then related to subsequent earnings. Veterans who had acquired transferable skills were not differentiated from those who did not, and if they had been differentiated, the results of chapter 7 might have been changed.

In this book's analysis of career patterns, individual choice figures most prominently. Here, the question "How well do U.S. labor markets work?" becomes simply "How do U.S. labor markets work?" In U.S. labor markets, a person's own choice would be critical if variables under the control of individuals were key to career success, namely the amount and type of education, training, and work experience one acquires. If, however, career trajectories are set in motion early in a person's working life and if these trajectories are hard to change due to the structure of the market (that is, the existence of internal labor markets in large firms with rigid promotional hierarchies, dualism in the external labor markets), individual choice would only be important early in a career.

Chapter 6 described the functioning of the labor market by developing a model of career adjustment which distinguished among three types of careers. The longitudinal record for young men was dissected into career segments and each 1–2 year period was categorized by the type of job change which occurred (if any) and the degree of growth in real earnings. The authors found that a typical young man demonstrated above-average growth in real earnings or an increase in work complexity ("career linearity") in 70 percent of the career segments we examined. In 15 percent of the career segments, a typical male worker showed neither above-average growth in real earnings, nor an increase in work complexity, and he remained either with the same employer or in the same occupation (in this career segment he was in a "steady state"). In less than 5 percent of the career segments did a young man experience less than average growth in real earnings, no increase in work complexity, and a change of employer and occupation (a "transitory" career change).

In a work force which was adjusting to a dramatic change in the structure of employment, one might expect a high number of transitory career changes as dislocated workers who sought to establish new careers accepted at least a temporary decline in earnings growth. The figures in this book did not reveal significant numbers of cases with these characteristics. The classic description of a dual labor market, where certain individuals are confined to jobs with low real earnings growth, few opportunities for advancement, and high turnover, was likewise not reflected in the figures. Instead, the high degree of interindustry mobility discovered in chapter 3, when combined with the picture described in chapter 6, implies that the market shifts which occur among young American men are largely directed at the establishment of increasingly rewarding careers, at least as measured by real earnings growth and increased job complexity. The changing structure of jobs in the U.S. economy seems to be having little measurable impact on the establishment of these career patterns.

The functioning of U.S. labor markets has up to this point been summarized through a series of descriptive indicators of performance. But each of the studies in this book goes beyond such description to an analysis of the causes of the separate phenomena which were studied. In each chapter, an analytical model was built to create a partial explanation of why labor markets function as they do. Through such models we can determine how uniformly labor markets treat individuals in the society, as described by race, income, age, education, and so forth.

A key policy consideration is how well blacks and other minorities adjust to new labor market conditions when their experience is compared to that of whites. Chapter 2 calculated the wage that dislocated workers could have expected, had they not lost their jobs (the predicted wage). Race was a significant explanation for the difference between the predicted wage and the actual wage earned by a dislocated worker. Nine months after losing a job, a dislocated black worker would have lost $1.35 per hour more than a white worker, *over and above* any discriminatory wage differential which would have occurred in the absence of a job dislocation. This degree of wage loss is substantial. Since the mean wage for blacks and whites was $7.85, the race differential is 17 percent of the mean wage earned by all young men.

In some respects, blacks appear to adjust equally as well as whites to changes in the structure of jobs, but in others, race makes quite a difference. Chapter 3 found that race was not an important variable for explaining the degree of interindustry mobility across the 1973–78 business cycle. All else constant, just as many blacks as whites left their industry of employment in 1973 and did not return by 1978. But in chapter 4, blacks were shown to be considerably *less* likely than whites to quit a job voluntarily and move. Since there was no significant difference by race in the probability that young men would quit jobs voluntarily and *not* move, blacks must be less inclined to search for jobs in new geographic locations. Though we might speculate on why blacks are less mobile, other research is needed to determine the reasons for the racial difference.

The results in chapters 3, 4, and 6 for the determinants of wage growth also show differences by race. Chapter 3 analyzed the effect of interindustry mobility on wage growth over the business cycle, chapter 4 addressed the impact of geographic mobility on wage growth, and chapter 6 measured wage growth as it related to differences in career patterns. Chapters 3 and 4 (tables 3–6 and 4–3) estimated a simple model of wage growth developed by Lazear, with age, education, race, and marital status held constant. The initial relationship found between race and wage growth (table 3–6, column 1) showed, surprisingly, that blacks experienced greater wage growth from 1973 to 1978 than whites. In referring to his similar results, Lazear called the findings "bizarre" but offered several possible explanations for them (Lazear, 1976, p. 557).

The combined results of chapters 3, 4, and 6 yield strong evidence that Lazear's surprising results derive from the effects of employer changes over time as individual work careers unfold. Lazear's results were replicated in our simplest model, when we controlled only for a young man's age prior to the beginning of the business cycle and his joblessness over the cycle (table 3–6, column 1). The results were different, once the control for labor market experience was refined. The first modification was to control for job tenure and the effect that mobility across industries would have on tenure (table 3–6, column 2). Once these disruptions in employer tenure were taken into account, race was not significantly related to wage growth. This result was reinforced in chapter 6 (table 6–3) when changes of employers were controlled in equations predicting wage growth over the early part of a young man's career. With this model, blacks had significantly slower wage growth than whites, a result which agrees with Diamond's estimates for the wage growth of NLS young men—also derived over a 5–10 year period of time (Diamond, 1983). Finally, in chapter 4 a wage-growth equation was estimated which controlled for the types of job changes that occur in conjunction with geographic mobility. With these changes controlled, blacks again showed slower wage growth than whites (table 4–3). We conclude that despite public policy emphasis on equal employment opportunity, the disadvantages that blacks face in the labor market become compounded over time by slower career advancement than that of comparable whites. This conclusion is supported in a different way in chapter 4, where blacks are shown to have significantly fewer voluntary transfers which involved a change of geographic location than are whites. Because such transfers often involve a promotion and increased job responsibilities, the racial difference gives further evidence of discrimination in career advancement based on race.

Race was also important in analyzing the effect of military service on the civilian work careers of blacks and whites. For blacks, service during the Vietnam War did not have a significant effect on subsequent civilian earnings, but for whites military service was linked with higher earnings. Race was not a significant factor in explaining whether skills acquired after the Vietnam War were transferable to the civilian sector, but blacks who served during the war were more likely to have unstable work careers following their term of service than were blacks who never served.

In the many partial models of labor market processes contained in this book, several interesting relationships were uncovered which enhance our understanding of how labor markets function. The degree of displacement which occurs within the U.S. economy, for instance, is quite unevenly distributed across industries, but where the displacement is highest depends in part on how we define displacement. If policymakers were to design displacement legislation based on the risk of involuntary job loss alone, they would target funds largely to the construction industry. Chapter 2 shows that construction workers run four times the risk of involuntary job loss than does the group of workers next most at risk, namely those working in durable goods industries (table 2–3). Nevertheless, over time young men are more strongly attached to the construction industry than to any other. Construction workers showed the lowest rate of interindustry mobility across the 1973–78 business cycle, and they did so despite a predicted wage growth that was lower than in any other sector of the economy (tables 3–2 and 3–7). Thus care must be taken in measuring displacement in the economy and in designing policy to deal with it.

Married men were expected to make different adjustments in the labor market depending on their wives' labor force attachment and earnings, but chapters 4 and 5 found little evidence to support these expectations. Though married men were less likely to move than were single men, neither their wives' labor force participation nor their earnings had any additional effect on the probability of geographic mobility (chapter 4). Likewise, even though a wife's income was statistically significant for predicting the duration of her husband's unemployment, the numerical impact was small. A 33 percent increase in a married woman's annual income raised the proportion of the year that her husband spent in unemployment only 3 percent (chapter 5).

If markets work as neoclassical economic theory predicts, human capital variables should be strongly related to a variety of labor market outcomes. In each of the chapters of this book, measures of human capital such as age, firm-specific work experience, education, and prior wage rates were related to several of the outcomes that young men experienced in the labor market. In chapter 2, for example, displaced workers who had higher predisplacement wage rates (and presumably more firm-specific skills) suffered larger postdisplacement wage losses. In chapter 3, job tenure was important in predicting interindustry mobility, and in chapter 6, age and education were strong determinants of the level of responsibility a young man achieved in his career. Yet the relationships between human capital variables and labor market outcomes were not always those expected.

A young man's wage rate and the characteristics of his local labor market were expected to affect his decision to move, and in many cases they did. Men who quit jobs voluntarily were more likely to move if they were from rural areas and if the area unemployment rate in 1970 was high, but neither of these factors affected the geographic mobility of displaced workers. Conversely, low-wage workers who were displaced were more likely to move than high-wage workers, but wage rates were not a factor in the decision to move among workers who were not displaced and quit their jobs voluntarily (table 4–2). Evidently labor markets affect decision making quite differently, depending on whether a person chooses to move voluntarily or is forced to consider moving due to job loss. In the former case, characteristics of the local labor market are important, whereas in the latter case, the financial condition of the family is key.

Both the descriptive analysis and the more detailed modeling of individual behavior contained in this book help establish the key characteristics of the U.S. labor market. In some ways, the market is highly fluid, but in others, the market is restricted in its ability to adjust to new conditions. On some measures, standard competitive economic theory makes appropriate predictions, but on others, a sociological view of a strongly structured market seems best. For example, the fluidity of the U.S. labor market is well documented in the data from chapter 3 on interindustry mobility. Yet young American men are much more mobile across major industries than they are geographically. When in a 5-year period only 10 percent of the most mobile age cohort of American men changes geographic location for economic reasons, one must question the degree to which U.S policy can rely on the geographic mobility of labor to help "clear the market." A policy of granting relocation assistance to workers is unlikely to speed their readjustment by very much. A community policy which aims for diversity in the industrial structure would be more desirable, allowing the high rate of interindustry mobility to facilitate economic adjustment and downplaying the role of geographic mobility in the adjustment process.

A second indication of the fluidity in U.S. markets is the finding from chapter 6 that a young man's first job or industry is not strongly related to his subsequent rate of wage growth, implying high mobility across jobs or other forces which equalize the advantages or disadvantages associated with a first job. Race, however, places a strong limitation on many men's mobility and long-run earnings. Americans have much work to do before markets treat blacks and whites equally. Blacks are less mobile geographically than whites and thus less able to adjust to changes in the locations of major U.S industries. Black young men exhibit careers with less rapid advancement than whites and show a less favorable pattern of wage rates over time. Black military veterans have not been awarded a wage advantage due to the credential that military service bestows, whereas white veterans have. And finally, black dislocated workers suffer considerably more wage loss following an involuntary job loss than do white workers.

In some cases, institutions did not have as large an impact on the fluidity of the market as we might have expected. For instance, providing unemployment insurance to workers displaced from jobs involuntarily had its intended effect: it eased readjustment without greatly prolonging the duration of unemployment. Likewise, the data in this book showed that the increased labor force participation of women is not a complicating factor in facilitating economic adjustment. Neither a wife's labor force participation nor her level of earnings had a significant impact on geographic mobility, and her earnings had negligible impact on the duration of unemployment her husband experienced.

Longitudinal data have been invaluable for answering a number of questions raised by this series of studies. This book reports on information gathered from the final year of surveys of a group of young men who were first interviewed in 1966. When first funded by the U.S. Department of Labor, the plans were for a longitudinal survey of only 5 years. Fortunately, the panel was extended for 10 additional years, allowing researchers to track employment experiences through to years when the young men were adult members of the labor force. We owe considerable thanks to the many men who remained in the survey for 15 years. Through their help, we have come to a better understanding of labor markets and have furnished much advice to policymakers regarding ways to improve labor market outcomes.

References

Diamond, Arthur. 1983. "The Distribution and Determinants of Individual Wage Profile Slopers." Columbus, Ohio: Center for Human Resource Research.

Gordon, David. 1972. *Theories of Poverty and Underemployment.* Lexington, Mass.: Lexington Books.

Hodson, Randy. 1984. "Companies, Industries, and the Measurement of Economic Segmentation." *American Sociological Review* 49 (June):335–348.

Jacoby, Sanford M. 1983. "Industrial Labor Mobility in Historical Perspective." *Industrial Relations* 22 (no. 2, Spring):261–282.

Kerr, Clark. 1954. "The Balkanization of Labor Markets." In Bakke, ed., *Labor Mobility and Economic Opportunity.* Cambridge, Mass.: MIT Press.

Lazear, Edward. 1976. "Age, Experience and Wage Growth." *American Economic Review* 66 (no. 4, September):548–558.

Parnes, Herbert S., et al. 1979. *From the Middle to the Later Years: Longitudinal Studies of the Preretirement and Postretirement Experience of Men.* Columbus, Ohio: Center for Human Resource Research.

U.S. Department of Commerce, Bureau of the Census. 1981. *Geographical Mobility: March 1975 to March 1980.* Current Population Reports, Series P-20, No. 368. Washington, D.C.: U.S. Government Printing Office, Dec.

———. 1973. *Occupation and Residence in 1965.* 1970 Census Subject Report PC(2)-7E. Washington, D.C.: U.S. Government Printing Office, June.

Index

Ability: measure of, 120, 121, 130n.11, 145n.8; postmilitary employment and, 5, 114, 115, 116, 129, 153

Age: and career mobility, 93–94, 98, 103, 157; and geographic mobility, 74, 151; and interindustry mobility, 44, 53, 150–151, 157; and unemployment, 9, 13, 60n.21, 81; and wage loss, 18, 25, 29, 74, 152. *See also* Experience; Tenure

Agricultural wage rates, 103, 120

Andrisani, P.J., 93, 95, 106

Armed Forces Qualification Test (AFQT), 135, 139, 141, 145n.8

Automobile industry: cyclical sensitivity of, 38, 49, 51; decline of, 7; and interindustry mobility, 4, 39, 40, 41, 48, 150; wage growth in, 4, 56

Bartel, Ann, 53, 64–67, 70, 78

Blacks. *See* Race

Blue-collar workers, 8, 15, 23, 26, 103

Borjas, George J., 55, 61n.22

Business cycle: industry sensitivity to, 38, 47, 48; and interindustry mobility, 45, 149, 150, 155; wage growth over, 55, 156

Career disruption, 18, 23, 92, 152

Career mobility, 19–112; choices and, 95, 153–154; factors affecting, 5, 91–109, 154, 157; models of, 91–93, 154; patterns of, 92–95, 154; structuralist theory of, 91–96, 108, 109; timing in, 8, 102, 107, 154; wage growth and, 67, 97–109 *passim,* 154, 155

Civilians: and veterans, occupational matches with, 135–137, 141; and Vietnam War, 113–114, 127, 178; wage growth of, 116, 117

Clerical occupations, 26, 103, 120

Collective bargaining. *See* Unions

Competition, perfect, 149–150, 158

Construction industry: and career mobility, 106; cyclical sensitivity of, 38, 49, 51; displacement in, 3, 11, 16, 38, 151, 156–157; and interindustry mobility, 40, 41, 47–48, 57, 157; job responsibility in, 103; unemployment insurance in, 51, 52; wage growth in, 4, 21, 25, 26, 55–56, 103, 120, 157

Costs: of career switching, 92, 101, 103; of changing firms, 73; of displacement, 2, 3, 7–9, 15–23, 79–89, 149, 152; of geographic mobility, 73; in interindustry mobility, 44, 58; of job search, 72, 85

Craft-internal labor market, 11, 16, 29

Craftsmen: interindustry mobility and, 47, 48; wages of, 26, 29, 120

Credentials effect, 114, 121, 127, 129n.5, 138. *See also* Military service, as credential

Data: census, 14, 150–151; from *Current Population Survey,* 1, 9, 87, 151. *See* National Longitudinal Surveys of Labor Market Experience

Data, People, Things, and Intelligence (DPTI) coefficient, 103, 106, 110n.3

De Vanzo, Julie, 64, 70, 74, 78

Discrimination: age, 19; in hiring practices, 150; racial, 25, 29, 155, 156; and veterans, 127, 129, 152

Displacement: advantages of, 32–33; age and, 9, 13; costs of, 2, 3, 7–9, 15–23, 32–33, 79–89, 149, 152; definition of, 1–2, 9–15; economic causes of, 7, 11, 13, 29, 33; legislation affecting, 1, 156, 157; and location, 33; problems in analysis of, 9, 149; rates of, 11, 13;

Displacement: *(continued)*
unemployment and, 15–18, 30–32, 149;
in various industries, 16, 156–157;
voluntary, 44, 66, 70, 71, 151, 157;
and wage loss, 3, 9, 18–23, 32, 151,
152
Driver, M.J., 92–111 *passim*
Dual labor market theory, 91, 96, 103,
150, 154
Durable goods manufacturing: and
interindustry mobility, 38, 41, 47, 48,
60n.16, 150, 156; wage growth in, 56

Economic climate: and displacement, 11,
13, 29, 33; and voluntary mobility,
44–45; and women, 86
Education: and career mobility, 5, 91,
93–109 *passim,* 154; and geographic
mobility, 67, 69–70, 71; human capital
theory on, 91, 93–95, 113, 129n.1;
and interindustry mobility, 44, 47,
60n.21; and job offers, 85; and job
responsibility, 157; parental, 115, 117;
and postmilitary employment, 114, 115,
137, 139; and probability of
unemployment, 81; and wage growth,
20, 26, 53, 74, 121; of wives, 82–83.
See also Training
Employers, 45, 46, 152, 153, 155
Employment: alternative, 25, 29, 32;
change in structure of, 154; duration
of, 114, 116, 120, 121; equal
opportunity, 5, 156; in past recessions,
38; of veterans, 113–132, 139, 141,
152, 153, 156
Experience: and career mobility, 91, 93–95,
98; and geographic mobility, 67; and
postmilitary employment, 114, 115,
121, 131n.25, 139; and wage growth,
73, 74

Families: and economic hardship, 78–89;
and geographic mobility, 4, 66; income
of, 3, 79; and wage loss, 26, 29
Firm size: and geographic mobility, 73, 74,
77; and postmilitary employment, 115,
117, 120, 121
Firm-specific skills, 8, 18, 19, 52, 72, 116,
140, 157

Geographic mobility, 63–78, 149, 150,
151, 157; determinants of, 66–71, 77,
151; and distance moved, 74–76, 77;
extent of, 64–66; job mobility and, 64,
68–69, 151, 158; policy implications of,
158; and race, 71, 77, 156, 158; study
of, 64–67, 70, 78; and wages,

67–69, 71–74, 77, 155, 157; and
working wives, 63, 64, 71, 77, 157,
158
Government policy: and displacement, 1,
2, 56, 79, 80, 88; and geographic
mobility, 158; and interindustry
mobility, 41, 43–44; 47; and labor
markets, 159; problems with, 156, 157;
on racial discrimination, 155, 156; and
unemployment compensation, 49,
51–52; and wage loss, 21, 23, 33
Government transfer payments, 4, 7, 49,
51–52, 79, 80, 81, 149, 152

Human capital: atrophy of, 25; and career
mobility, 93–95, 98, 106, 108;
firm-specific, 8, 18, 19, 72, 116, 140,
157; and the military, 113, 115, 133,
134, 137; theory of, 91, 93, 113, 114,
129n.1, 129n.8, 139, 157; and
unemployment, 81–83, 87

Income: sources of, 3, 79, 86, 152;
unearned, 80, 82, 85
Income replacement ratio, 80, 81, 85,
88n.2
Industries: and career mobility, 96, 98,
104, 106, 107; cyclically sensitive,
47–51; declining, 7, 33, 43, 44; and
interindustry mobility, 4, 45, 48–49;
and postmilitary employment, 115; and
wage growth, 27, 29, 33, 103
Information costs, 74–76
Interfirm mobility, 73, 149
Interindustry mobility, 37–62, 149, 150;
determinants of, 41–47, 54, 150–151,
155–157; between firms, 73, 149; vs.
geographical mobility, 151, 158;
involuntary, 44–45; rates of, 39–41;
in various industries, 39, 40, 41, 47,
48, 57, 150, 157; and wage growth,
52–56, 154, 155

Jacobs, J., 93, 96, 107
Job search: costs of, 18, 72, 85; and
interindustry mobility, 54; model of,
79–80, 85, 152; subsidization of, 80,
82

Knowledge of the World of Work
(KOWW), 120, 121, 130n.11, 130n.12

Labor market: adjustments in, 3, 4, 8,
150–157; characteristics of, 157–158;
models of, 155–156; size of, 44, 47, 67,
71; structure of, 23, 95–96, 98, 106,

107, 150, 154, 158; theory of, 149–159, 158

Law, careers in, 95, 96, 107

Layoffs: and geographic mobility, 66, 70, 71, 73, 75; and interindustry mobility, 54; reasons for, 44, 45

Lazear, Edward, 53, 60n.18, 60n.20, 155–156

"Leavers": and interindustry mobility, 41–49, 53–55, 56–58; and unemployment, 15, 16

Linear career pattern, 92–103 *passim,* 109, 154

Manufacturing industries, 103, 106; cyclical sensitivity of, 7, 51; interindustry, 38, 39, 40, 41, 57; unemployment insurance in, 52; wage rate in, 26, 29, 120

Marital status, 60n.20, 60n.21, 67, 70, 80, 139, 157. *See also* Wives, working

Medical career, 95, 96

Military service: advantages of, 121, 128, 129; as credential, 5, 115, 120, 129, 152, 153; long-run effects of, 120, 121, 127, 128, 129; noncompletion of, 135–141 *passim;* short-run effects of, 120, 129n.4; types of training in, 133, 144; and wage growth, 114, 116, 120, 121, 127–129, 141, 149, 152, 153

Military-civilian skill transfer, 133–147; factors affecting, 134–137, 139, 140, 153; and occupational match, 5, 135–137, 141, 144

Mincer, J., 106, 129n.1, 129n.8

Mining industry, 103, 106, 120

Models, 154, 155, 156: of career mobility, 91–93; of displacement costs, 15–32; of geographic mobility, 67–74; of interindustry mobility, 41–49, 52–56; job search, 79–80, 83–87; of postmilitary employment, 114–115, 137–141

Motivation, 88n.4, 92–93, 95, 98, 102, 106, 108

Moves, 64, 66, 67, 71–76. *See also* Geographic mobility

National Longitudinal Surveys of Labor Market Experience (NLS): and analysis of U.S. labor market, 150–159; on displaced workers, 10, 13–14, 16; on effects of military service, 114, 115, 116, 130n.12, 130n.13; on household income, 79; on mobility, 39–40, 64, 65; structure of, 3, 6n; on unemployment, 81, 84, 87

Nondurable goods manufacturing, 38, 40, 41, 47, 48, 60n.16

Occupational match, military-civilian, 135–144 *passim,* 153

Organization position, 73, 74

Private sector, 11, 14

Professional/managerial occupation, 32, 47, 48, 95, 96, 103, 150

Protectionism, 43–44

Protestant work ethic, 95

Public service sector, 103, 120

Race: and career mobility, 98, 99, 107, 108; and geographic mobility, 4, 67, 70, 71, 156; and interindustry mobility, 47, 155; and job offers, 85; and military skill transfer, 5, 135, 137, 139–140; and postmilitary employment, 114–121 *passim,* 129, 131n.22, 152, 153, 156; and public policy, 156; and unemployment, 60n.21, 80, 81, 149; and voluntary transfer, 71, 156; and wage rate, 25, 29, 60n.20, 74, 103, 107, 155, 158

Real estate industry, 103

Recession: and geographic mobility, 64; and interindustry mobility, 39–41, 48; of 1975, 37, 38, 64; of 1981–1982, 37, 38; and unemployment, 3, 49–52; and wage growth, 52–56

Reservation, wage, 85, 121, 131n.23

Residence: and career mobility, 96, 98; and postmilitary employment, 115, 117, 120, 121, 140; and wage growth, 33. *See also* Standard Metropolitan Statistical Area residence

Responsibility, job, 97, 103, 109, 154, 156, 157

Retraining programs, 2, 47

"Returners," 41, 49, 55, 59n.5

Sales occupations, 26, 103

Screening effect. *See* Credentials effect

Seniority, 13, 25, 29, 45. *See also* Age; Tenure

Service industry: and interindustry mobility, 4, 40, 41, 47, 150; occupations in, 120, 141; and unemployment, 15, 49, 51

Skills: firm-specific, 8, 18, 19, 52, 72, 116, 140, 157; and involuntary mobility, 45; transfer of, 32, 44, 53; and wage growth, 73. *See also* Military-civilian skill transfer; Training

Social welfare payments, 79, 81

Spiral career pattern, 92–93, 109n.1

Standard Metropolitan Statistical Area (SMSA) residence, 19, 20, 27, 32, 81, 85, 115; and career mobility, 98, 108; and military-civilian skill transfer, 140, 141; and wage rate, 103, 120–121; and worktime, 121
Status: job, 96, 102, 103, 106, 107; occupational, 96, 98, 102, 103, 107; parental, 103, 107, 108; socioeconomic, 81, 139
"Stayers," 41, 48, 55, 59n.5
Steady-state career pattern, 92–109 *passim,* 154
Steel industry: cyclical sensitivity of, 49, 51; decline of, 7; and interindustry mobility, 3, 38–41, 48, 150; unemployment insurance in, 51; wage growth in, 56
Structuralist theory, 91–96 *passim,* 108, 109, 150, 154

Technology, 1, 2, 7
Tenure: advantages of, 8; and interindustry mobility, 44–49, 55, 59n.13, 156, 157; and military skill transfer, 140, 141; and wage rates, 25, 29, 30, 55, 74
Timing, career, 8, 102, 107, 154
Training, 81, 85, 154; human capital theory of, 91, 93–95, 113, 129n.1; military, 115, 121, 133–139, 144, 153; on-the-job, 32, 53, 91, 93, 106, 145n.2. *See also* Education
Transfers: distance of, 74–76; and geographic mobility, 72, 157; involuntary, 64, 65–66, 70, 72, 73; vs. movers, 71–74; probability of, 67–68; voluntary, 64–66, 70, 72, 73, 74, 156; working wives and, 66–67, 70
Transitory career pattern, 92–109 *passim,* 154
Transportation industry, 103

Unemployment, 79, 88, 149; and career mobility, 98, 103, 107; costs of (*See* Costs); and displacement, 15–18, 30–32; duration of, 83–88, 152; and geographic mobility, 4, 67, 71; households experiencing, 80–81; and interindustry mobility, 54; probability

of, 81–83, 87; and working wives, 79–98 *passim,* 157, 158
Unemployment insurance: effect of, 3, 4, 79, 86, 152, 158; and interindustry mobility, 49, 51–52, 57–58; and unemployment duration, 4, 88, 158
Unions: and interindustry mobility, 44, 47, 48, 57, 59n.8, 150; and military-civilian skill transfer, 140, 141; and postmilitary employment, 115, 117, 120, 121
Upward mobility, 101, 103–106
Utilities industry, 103, 150

Veterans, 116, 117, 130n.18. *See also* Military-civilian skill transfer
Vietnam War, 1, 3, 5, 113, 114, 127, 129, 133, 152
Voluntary job loss, 44, 66, 69–75 *passim,* 151, 157

Wage growth: and career mobility, 67, 97–98, 102, 103, 107, 109, 154, 155; in construction industry, 4, 21, 25, 26, 55–56, 103, 120, 157; and first job, 158; and geographic mobility, 67–69, 71–74, 77, 155, 157; and interindustry mobility, 52–56, 154, 155; Lazear's model of, 53, 60n.18, 60n.20, 155–156; and military service, 114, 116, 120, 121, 127–128, 141, 149, 152, 153; and race, 25, 29, 60n.20, 74, 103, 107, 155, 158
Wage loss: and age, 18, 25, 29, 74, 152; determinants of, 23–32; following displacement, 3, 9, 18–23, 32, 151, 152; methods of estimating, 19–20, 33–35; and predisplacement wages, 26, 29, 157; variance in, 21–22, 33
White-collar workers, 15, 23, 29, 32
Wives, working, 66, 79, 80; education of, 82–83; and geographic mobility, 4, 66–67, 70, 71, 157, 158; and husband's unemployment, 85–87, 88, 149, 152, 157

Young Men's Cohort, 3, 87, 114, 115, 116, 130n.12, 130n.13
Youth Cohort, 3, 133, 134

About the Authors

Stephen M. Hills has been at The Ohio State University since 1977. He is currently associate professor of management and human resources, and he served as acting director of the Center for Human Resource Research in 1983–84. He has published articles on the long-run effects of teenage unemployment, the effects of unemployment insurance on the duration of unemployment, how skilled workers acquire their training, and factors influencing individual attitudes toward unionization. He was formerly a faculty member at the University of British Columbia, where he served both as a mediator and an arbitrator. His academic training is in economics and industrial relations.

David Ball, research associate, Center for Human Resource Research, The Ohio State University, is currently working as a computer programmer. Prior to this, he did research for the Utah Department of Employment Security on local labor market measures of the unemployment rate. His academic training is in human resource management.

Ronald J. D'Amico, research consultant at SRI International, Menlo Park, California, has published articles related to dual labor market thoery, the career development of young men, and the consequences and determinants of the social organization of the labor market. His academic training is in sociology.

Jeff Golon, research associate, Center for Human Resource Research, The Ohio State University, is presently serving as archivist for NLS data. His academic training is in political science.

John L. Jackson is currently credit scoring manager, Firestone Tire and Rubber, Cleveland, Ohio. His academic training is in labor economics.

Janina C. Latack, assistant professor of management and human resources, The Ohio State University, has published articles on human resource management and organizational behavior. She is interested in work stress, the management of job loss, the success of women apprentices in the construction trades, and the career mobility of women workers. Her academic training is in organizational behavior.

Lisa M. Lynch, assistant professor of management, Massachusetts Institute of Technology, has published articles on unemployment among British youth, strike frequency in British coal mining, and the impact of Title VII of the U.S Civil Rights Act on professional women. She was formerly a faculty member at The Ohio State University and is trained in labor economics.

Stephen Mangum, assistant professor of management and human resources, The Ohio State University, has published articles on labor exchanges, job search, youth unemployment, and adult education and training. He has served as a manpower planner and survey specialist for the U.S. Agency for International Development and has done contract work for the Army Research Institute. His academic training is in labor economics.

David Shapiro, associate professor of economics, Pennsylvania State University, has published articles and monographs on the labor force attachment, work expectations, and earnings of women, as well as on the wage effects of unions and the economic aspects of education. He has done research on demography and education in Africa and is currently in Zaire, sponsored by the U.S. Agency for International Development. His academic training is in labor economics.